D1127680

WONDER WOMAN

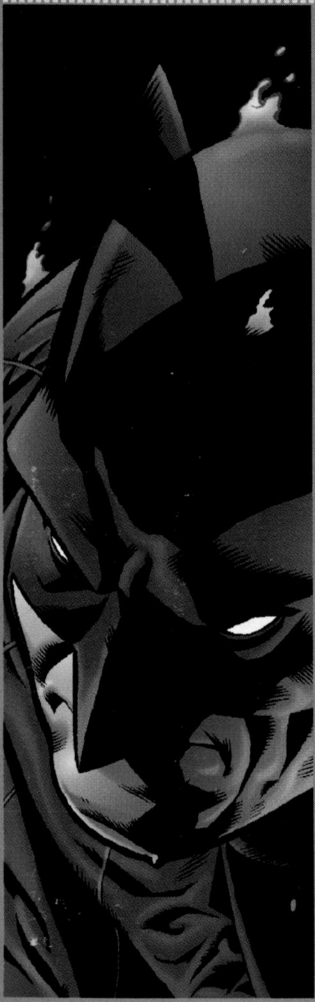

WONDER WOMAN: THE HIKETEIA.
Published by DC Comics,
1700 Broadway, New York, NY 10019.

Printed in Canada.

DC Comics. A division of Warner Bros.-
An AOL Time Warner Company

Cover painting by J.G. Jones
Logo design by Glenn Parsons

WONDER WOMAN®
THE HIKETEIA

WRITER
Greg Rucka

PENCILLER
J. G. Jones

INKER
Wade von Grawbadger

LETTERER
Todd Klein

COLORIST
Dave Stewart

WONDER WOMAN
CREATED BY
WILLIAM MOULTON MARSTON

I offer myself in supplication,
I come without protection.
I come without means.
Without honor, without hope,
With nothing but myself
to beg for protection.

In your shadow will I serve.
By your breath will I breathe.
By your words will I speak.
By your mercy will I live.

With all my heart
with everything I can offer
I beg you, in Zeus's name,
who watches over all supplicants:

ACCEPT MY PLEA.

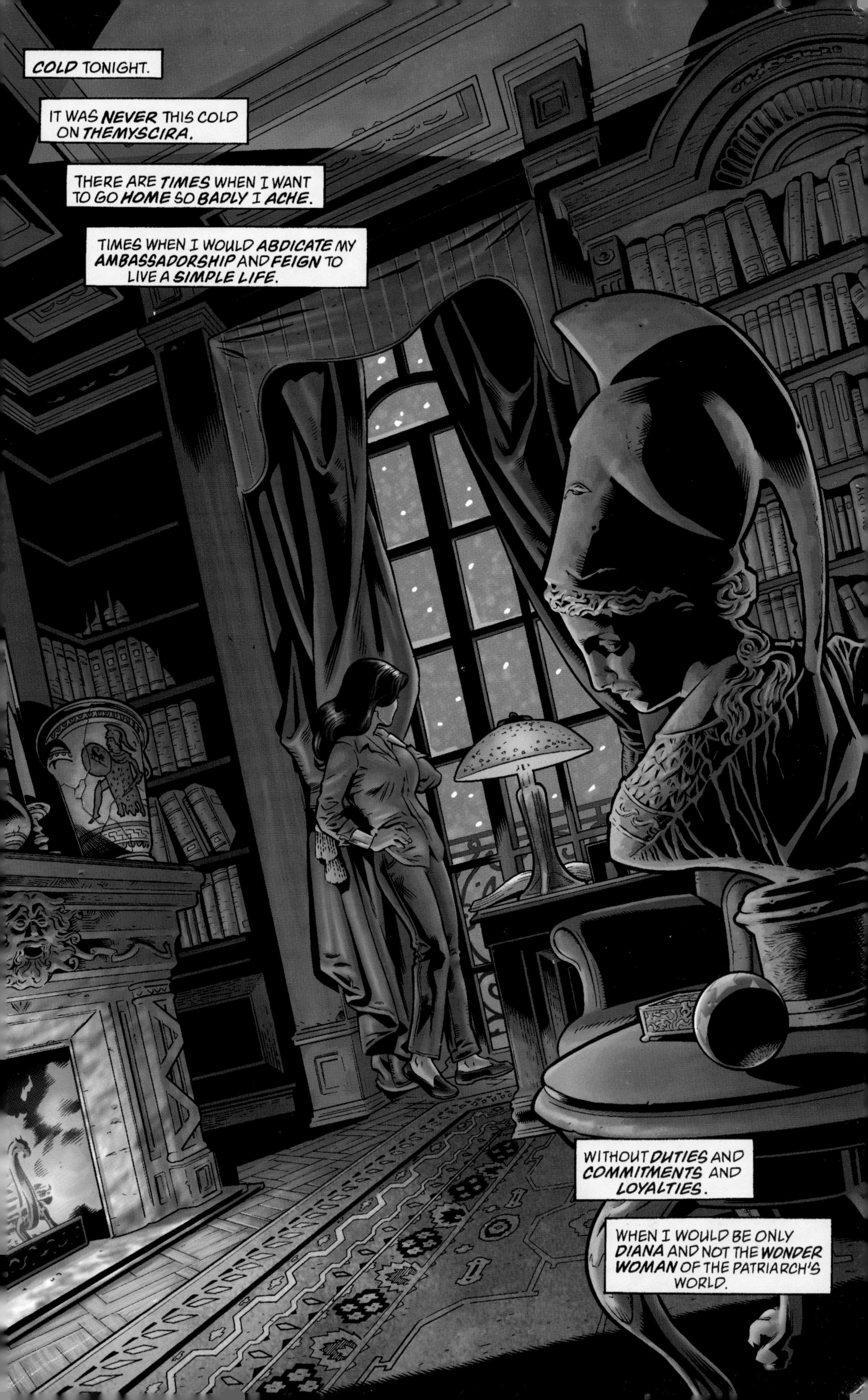
COLD TONIGHT.
IT WAS NEVER THIS COLD ON THEMYSCIRA.
THERE ARE TIMES WHEN I WANT TO GO HOME SO BADLY I ACHE.
TIMES WHEN I WOULD ABDICATE MY AMBASSADORSHIP AND FEIGN TO LIVE A SIMPLE LIFE.
WITHOUT DUTIES AND COMMITMENTS AND LOYALTIES.
WHEN I WOULD BE ONLY DIANA AND NOT THE WONDER WOMAN OF THE PATRIARCH'S WORLD.

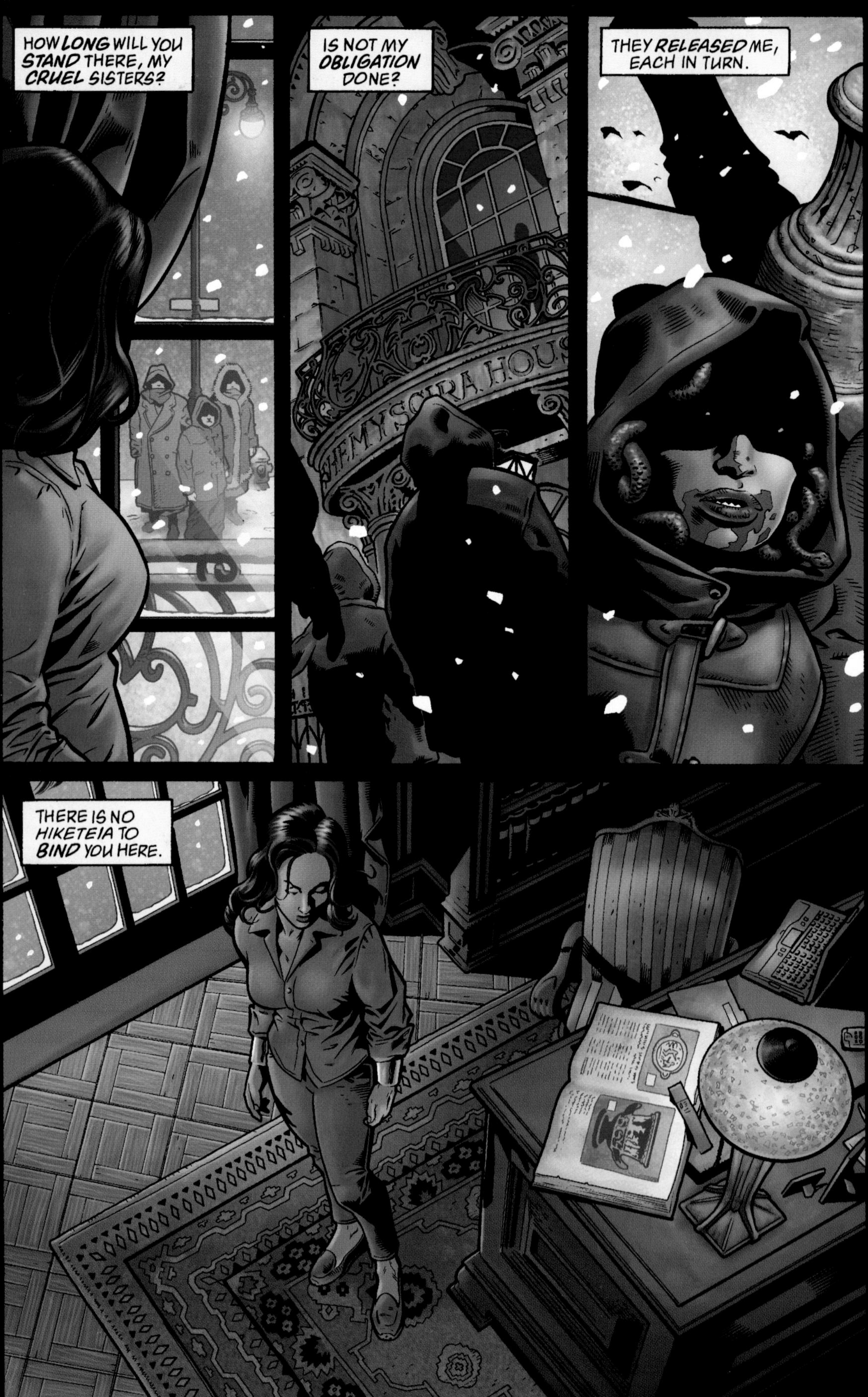
HOW LONG WILL YOU STAND THERE, MY CRUEL SISTERS?
IS NOT MY OBLIGATION DONE?
THEMYSCIRA HOUS
THEY RELEASED ME, EACH IN TURN.
THERE IS NO HIKETEIA TO BIND YOU HERE.

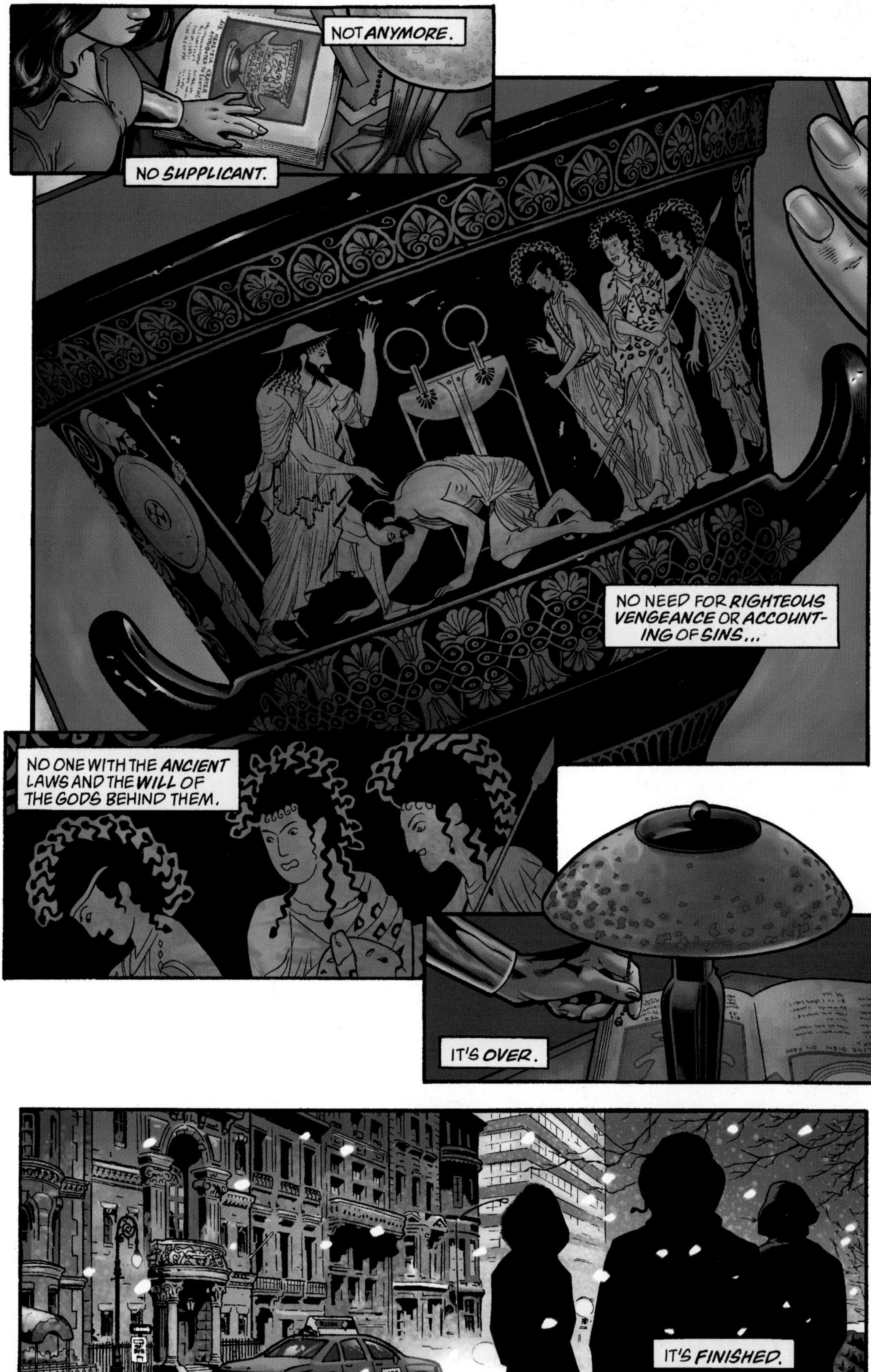
NOT ANYMORE.
NO SUPPLICANT.
NO NEED FOR RIGHTEOUS VENGEANCE OR ACCOUNTING OF SINS...
NO ONE WITH THE ANCIENT LAWS AND THE WILL OF THE GODS BEHIND THEM.
IT'S OVER.
IT'S FINISHED.

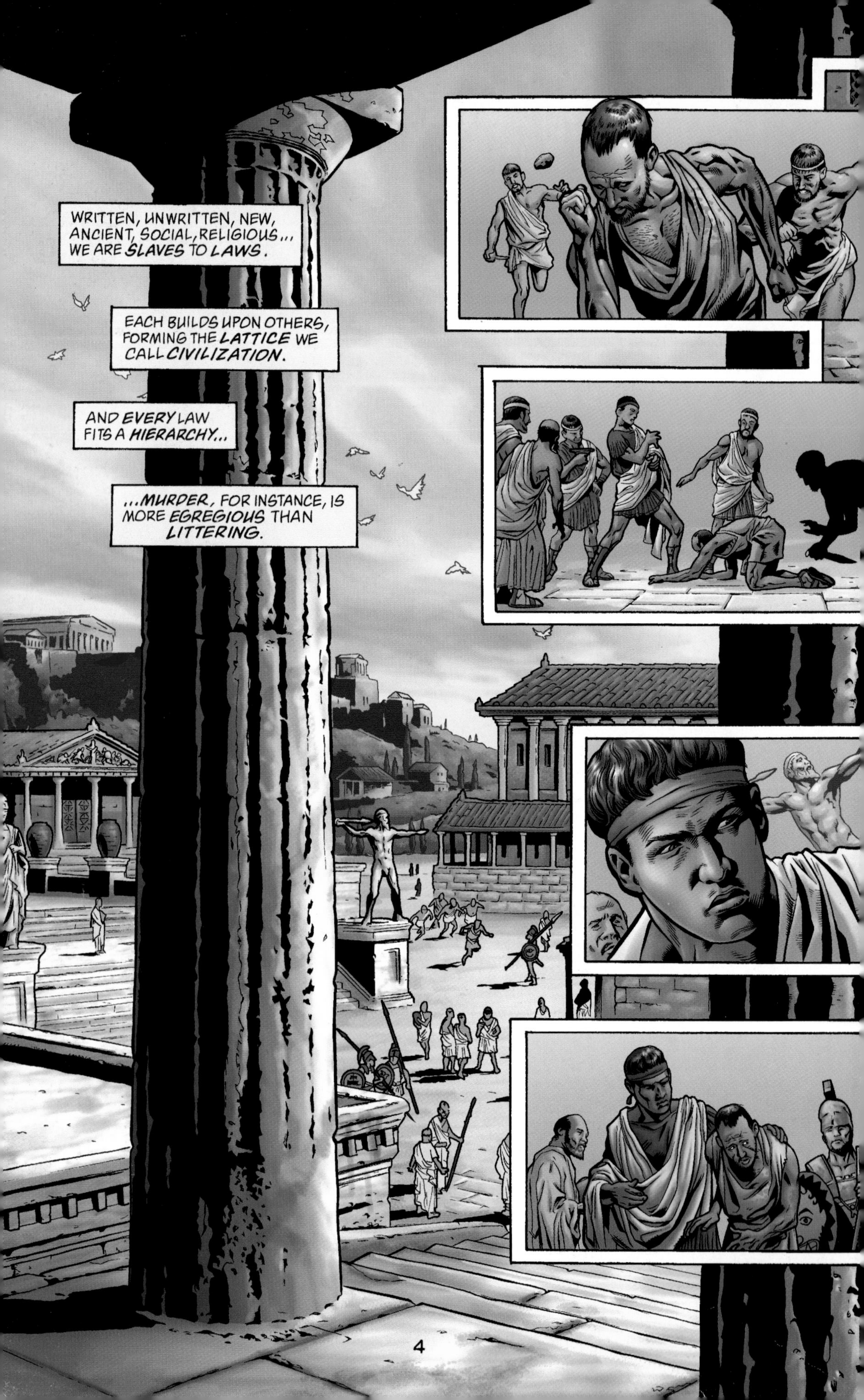
WRITTEN, UNWRITTEN, NEW, ANCIENT, SOCIAL, RELIGIOUS... WE ARE SLAVES TO LAWS.
EACH BUILDS UPON OTHERS, FORMING THE LATTICE WE CALL CIVILIZATION.
AND EVERY LAW FITS A HIERARCHY...
...MURDER, FOR INSTANCE, IS MORE EGREGIOUS THAN LITTERING.

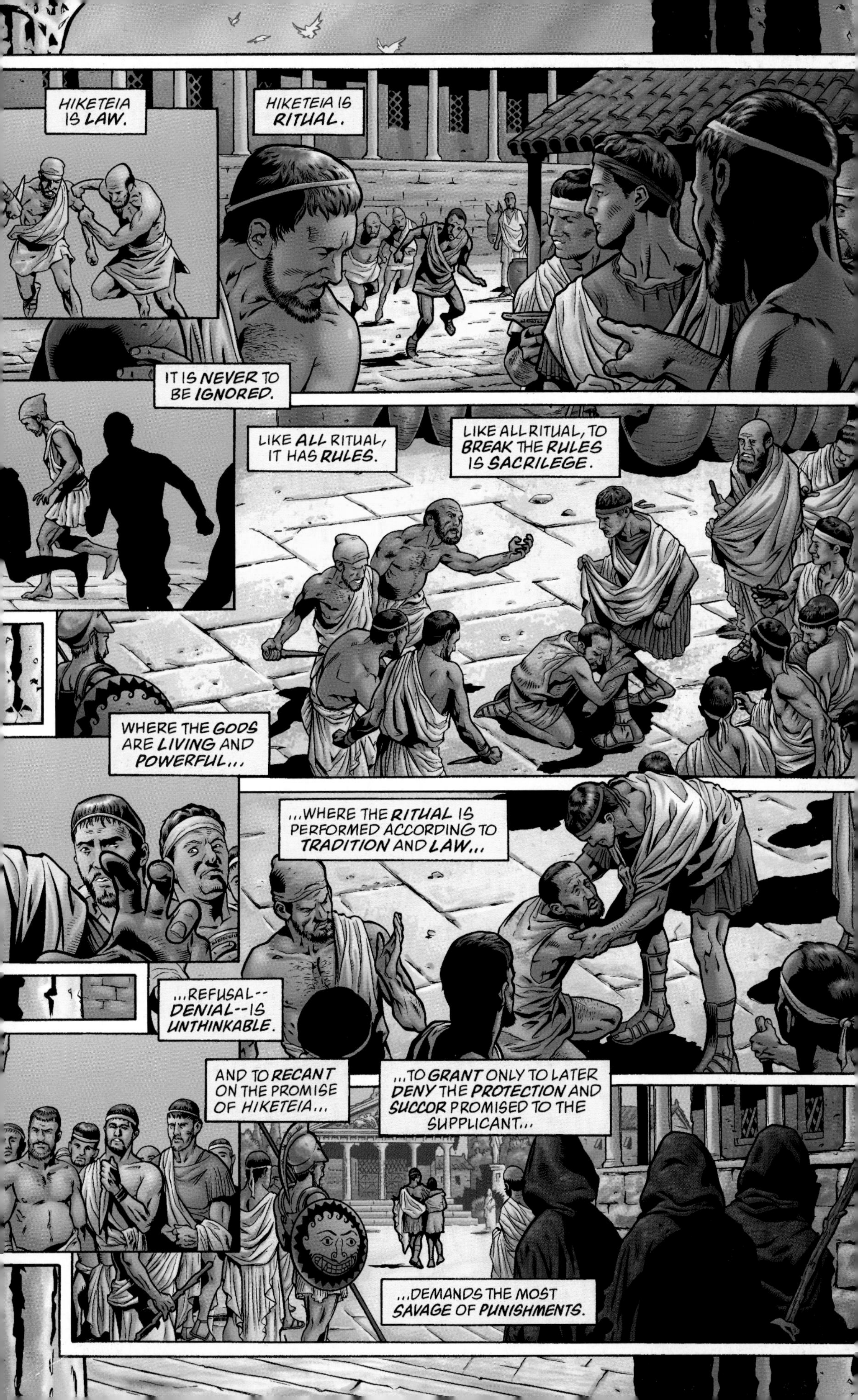
HIKETEIA IS LAW.
HIKETEIA IS RITUAL.
IT IS NEVER TO BE IGNORED.
LIKE ALL RITUAL, IT HAS RULES.
LIKE ALL RITUAL, TO BREAK THE RULES IS SACRILEGE.
WHERE THE GODS ARE LIVING AND POWERFUL...
...WHERE THE RITUAL IS PERFORMED ACCORDING TO TRADITION AND LAW...
...REFUSAL--DENIAL--IS UNTHINKABLE.
AND TO RECANT ON THE PROMISE OF HIKETEIA...
...TO GRANT ONLY TO LATER DENY THE PROTECTION AND SUCCOR PROMISED TO THE SUPPLICANT...
...DEMANDS THE MOST SAVAGE OF PUNISHMENTS.

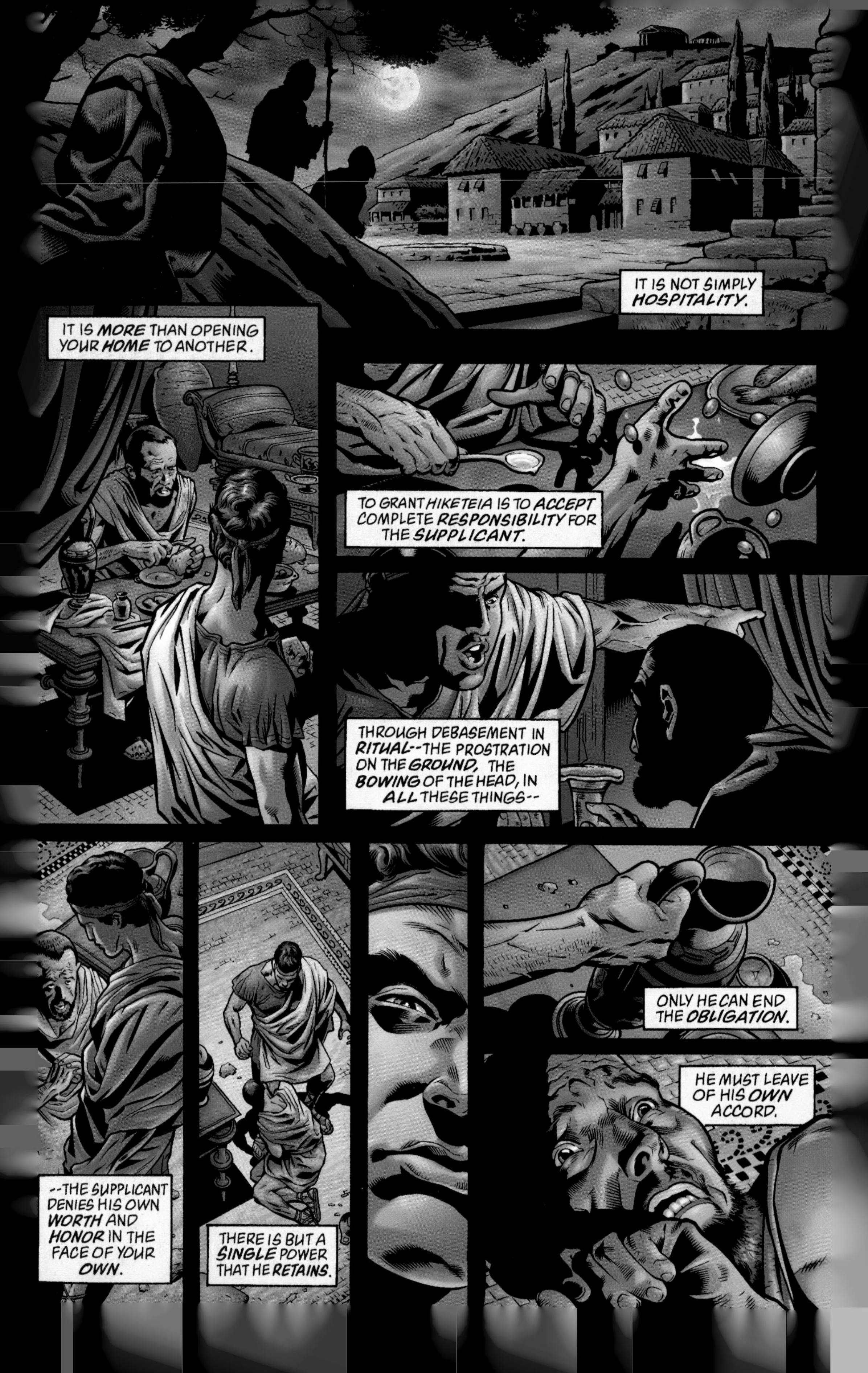
IT IS NOT SIMPLY HOSPITALITY.
IT IS MORE THAN OPENING YOUR HOME TO ANOTHER.
TO GRANT HIKETEIA IS TO ACCEPT COMPLETE RESPONSIBILITY FOR THE SUPPLICANT.
THROUGH DEBASEMENT IN RITUAL--THE PROSTRATION ON THE GROUND, THE BOWING OF THE HEAD, IN ALL THESE THINGS--
--THE SUPPLICANT DENIES HIS OWN WORTH AND HONOR IN THE FACE OF YOUR OWN.
THERE IS BUT A SINGLE POWER THAT HE RETAINS.
ONLY HE CAN END THE OBLIGATION.
HE MUST LEAVE OF HIS OWN ACCORD.

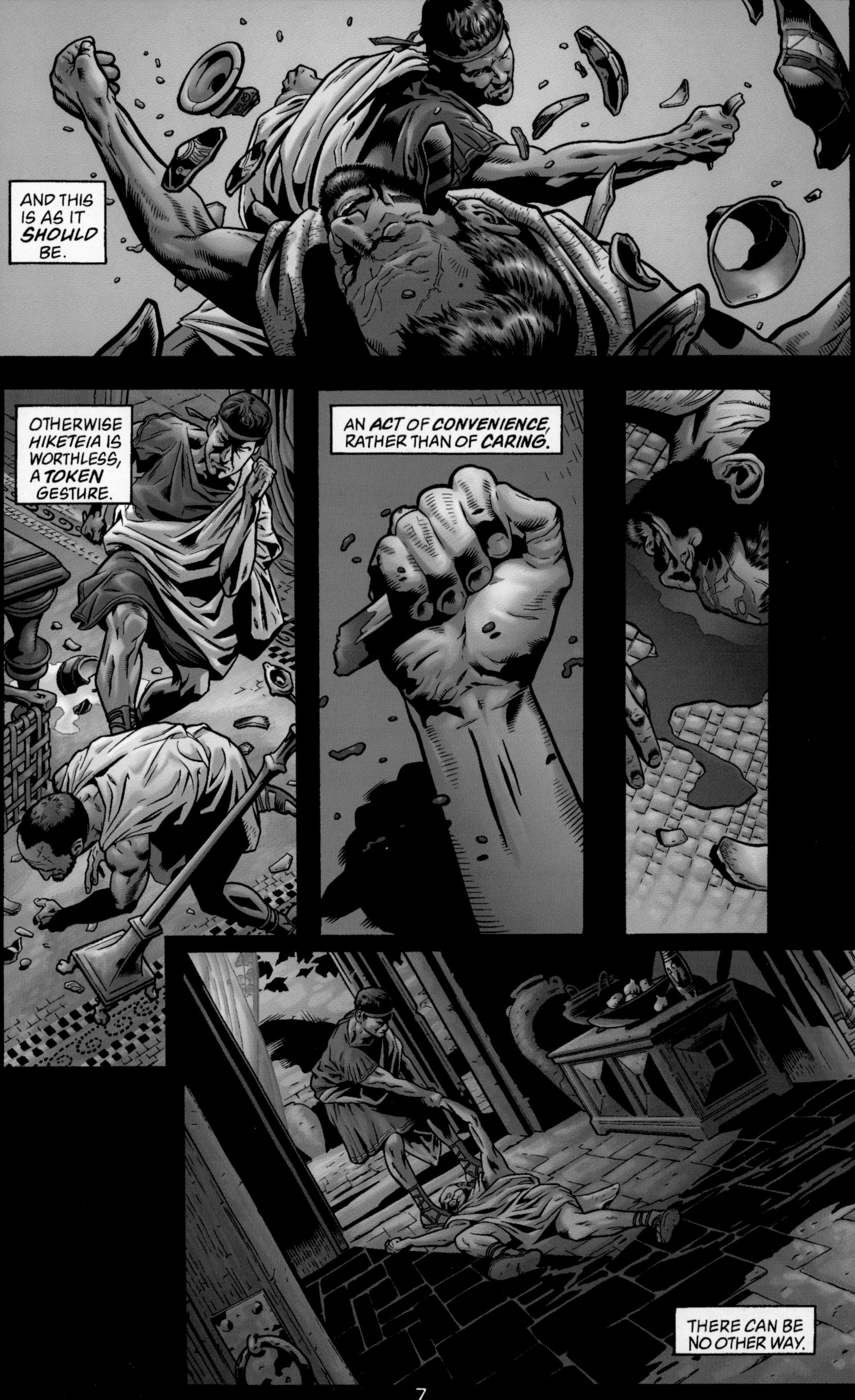
AND THIS IS AS IT SHOULD BE.
OTHERWISE HIKETEIA IS WORTHLESS, A TOKEN GESTURE.
AN ACT OF CONVENIENCE, RATHER THAN OF CARING.
THERE CAN BE NO OTHER WAY.

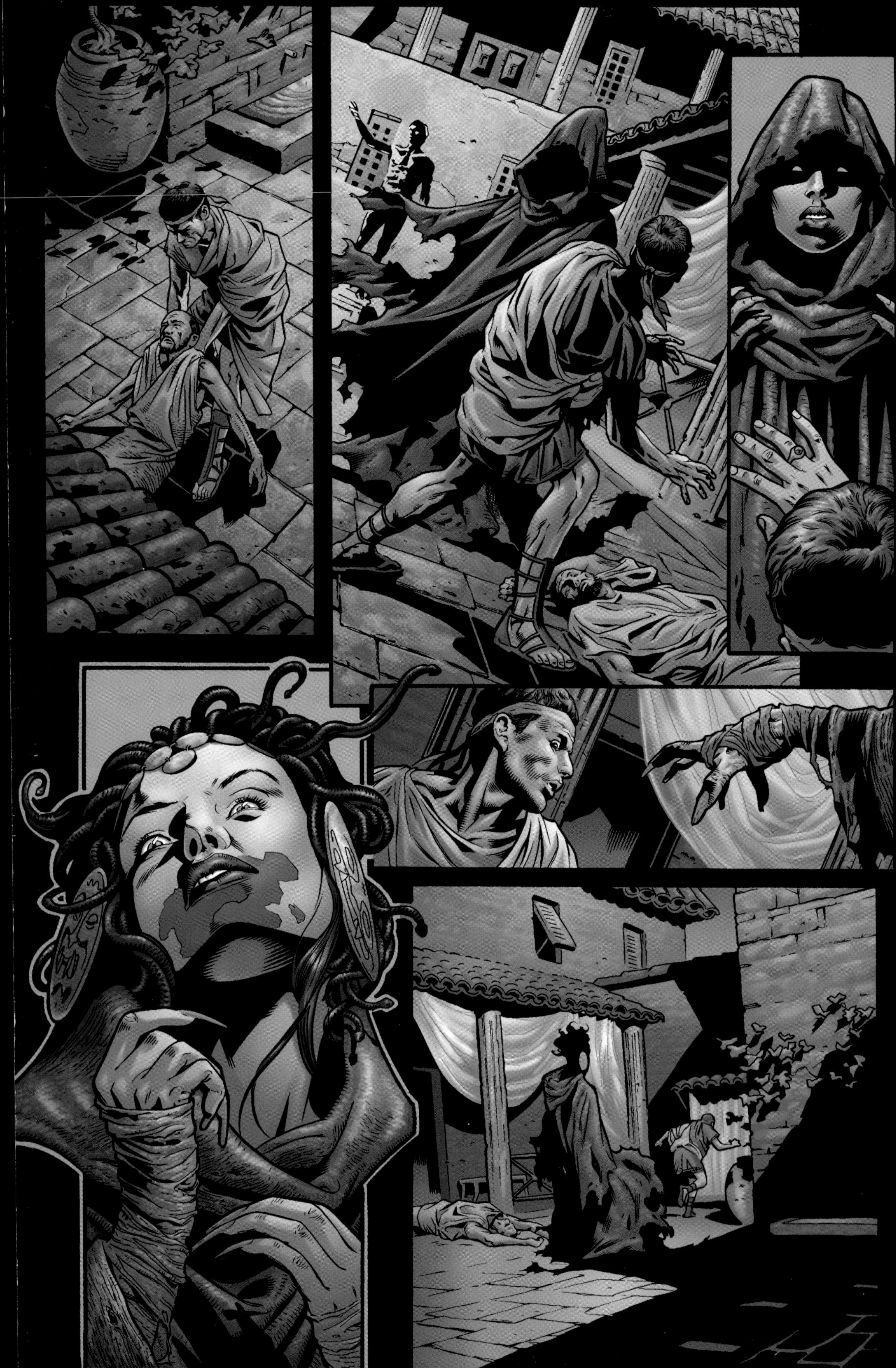

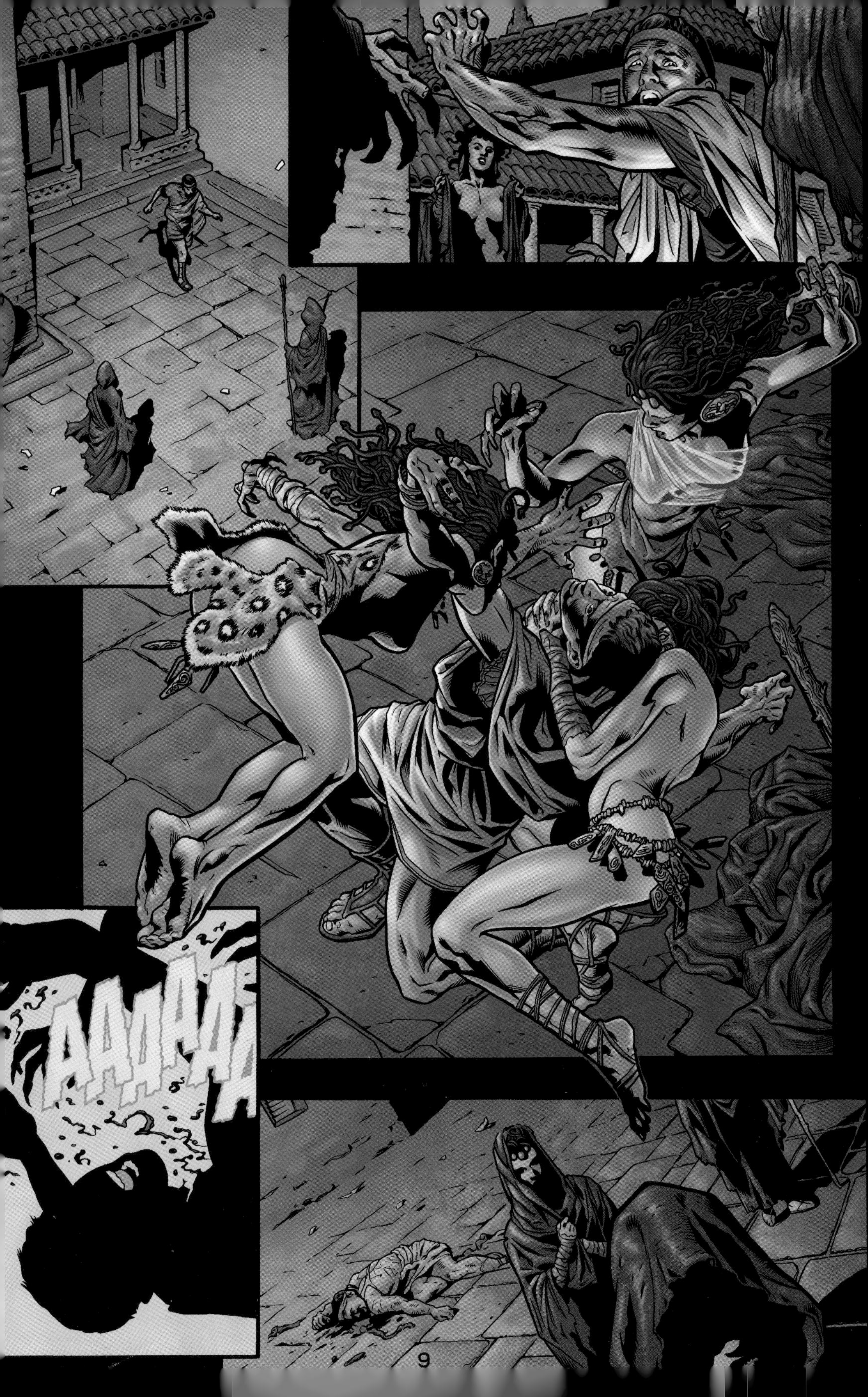
AAAAA

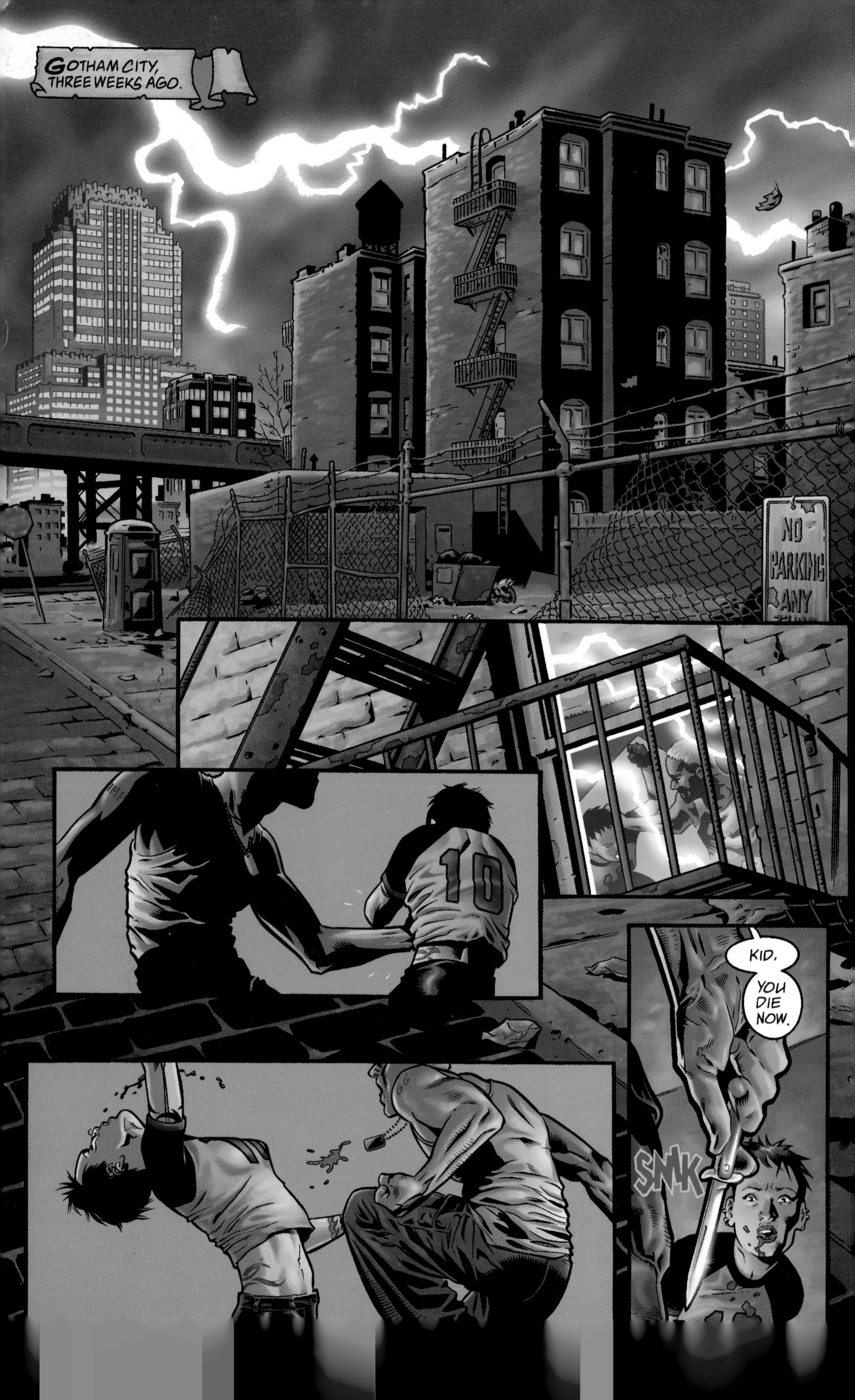
GOTHAM CITY, THREE WEEKS AGO.
NO PARKING ANY
KID.
YOU DIE NOW.
SNIK

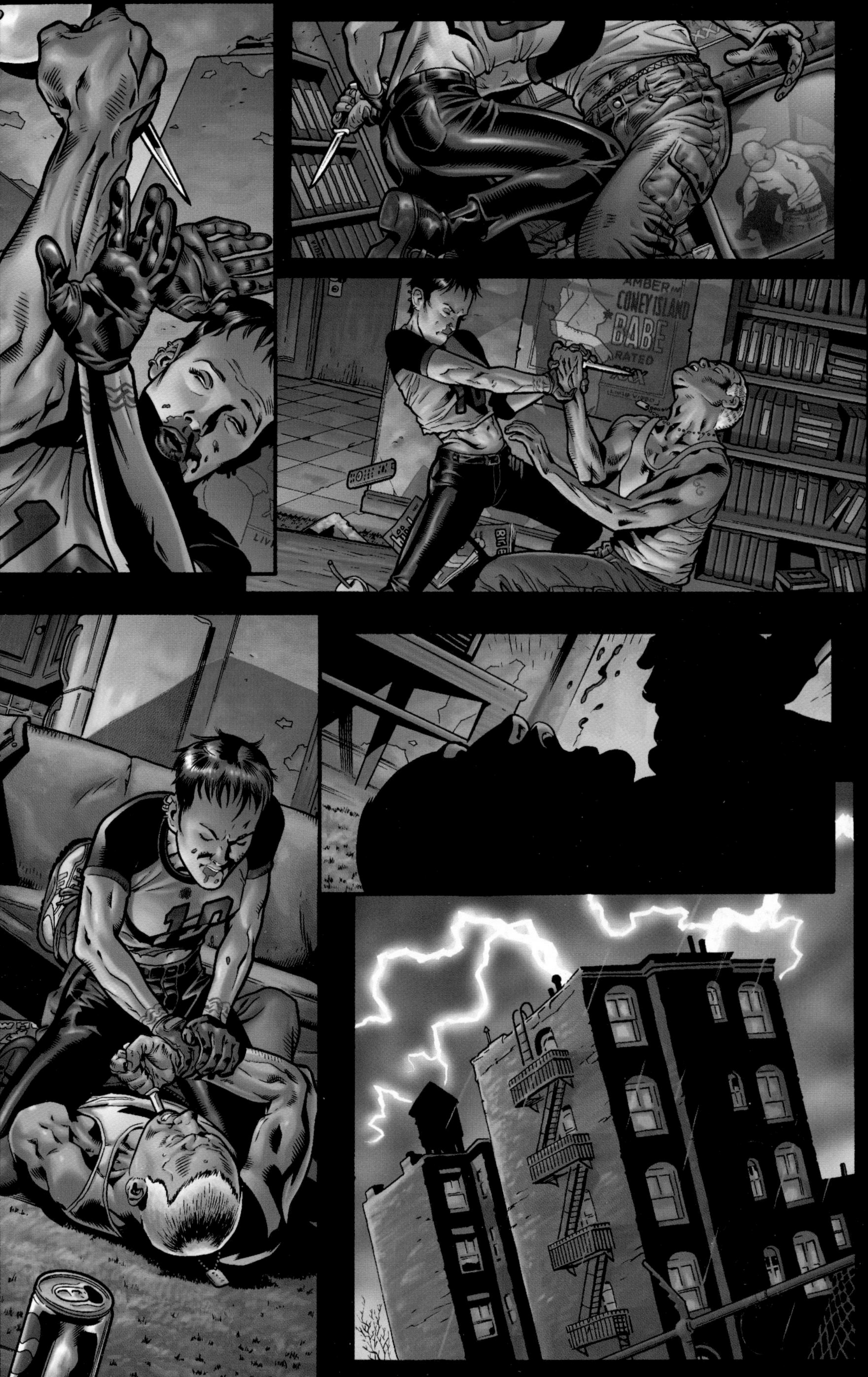
AMBER IN
CONEY ISLAND
BABE
RATED

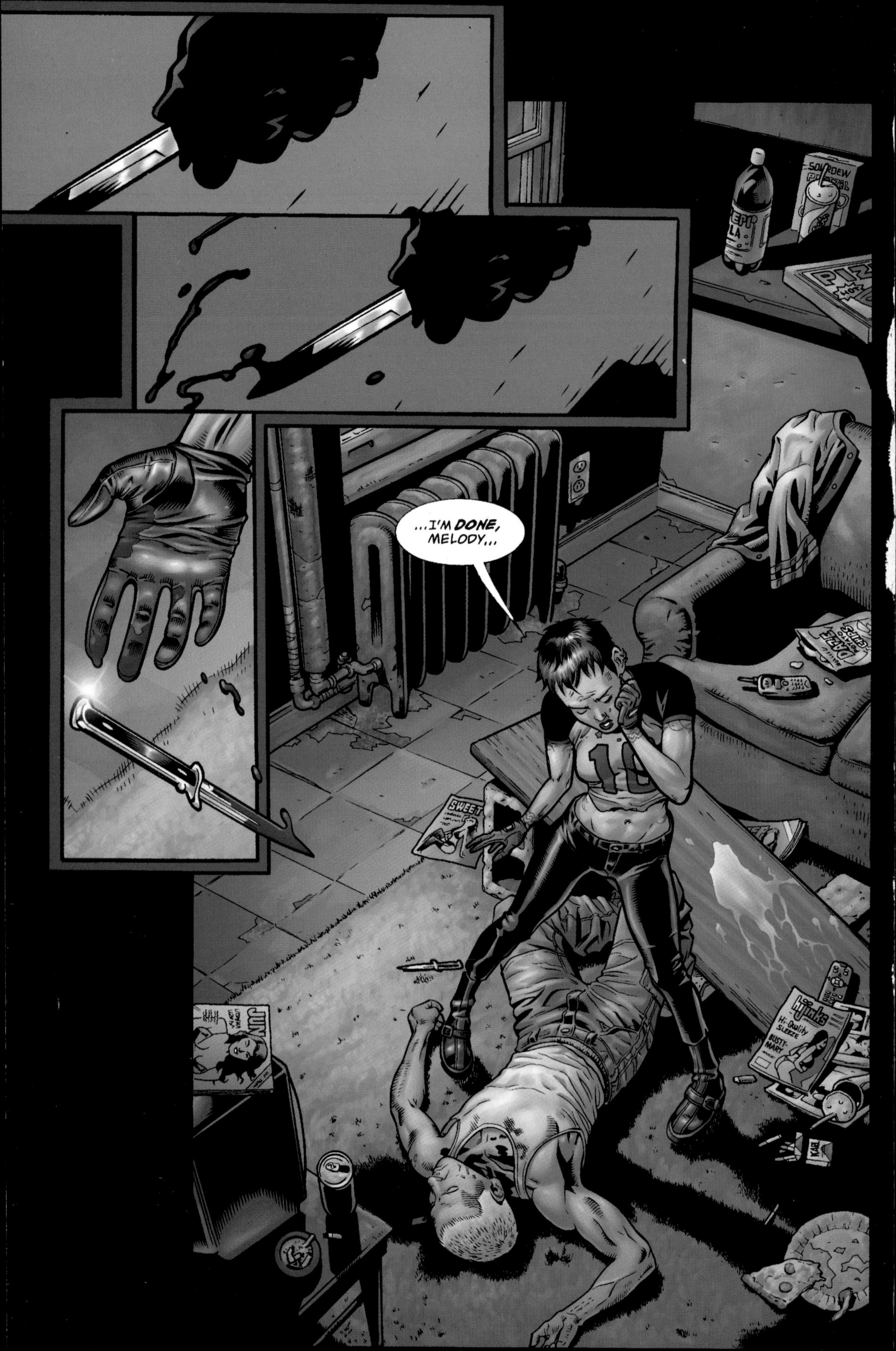
...I'M DONE, MELODY...

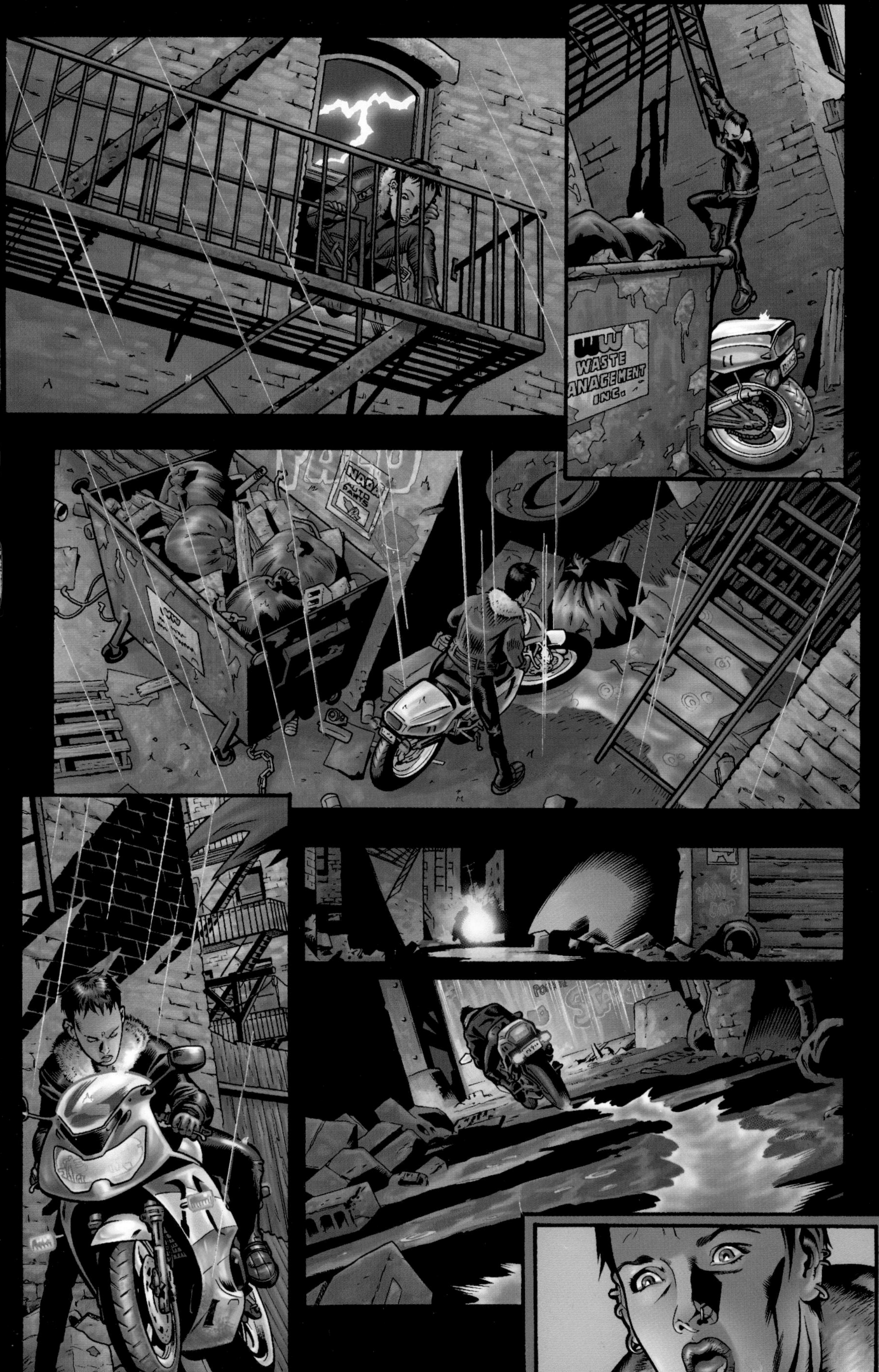
WW
WASTE
ANAGEMENT
INC.

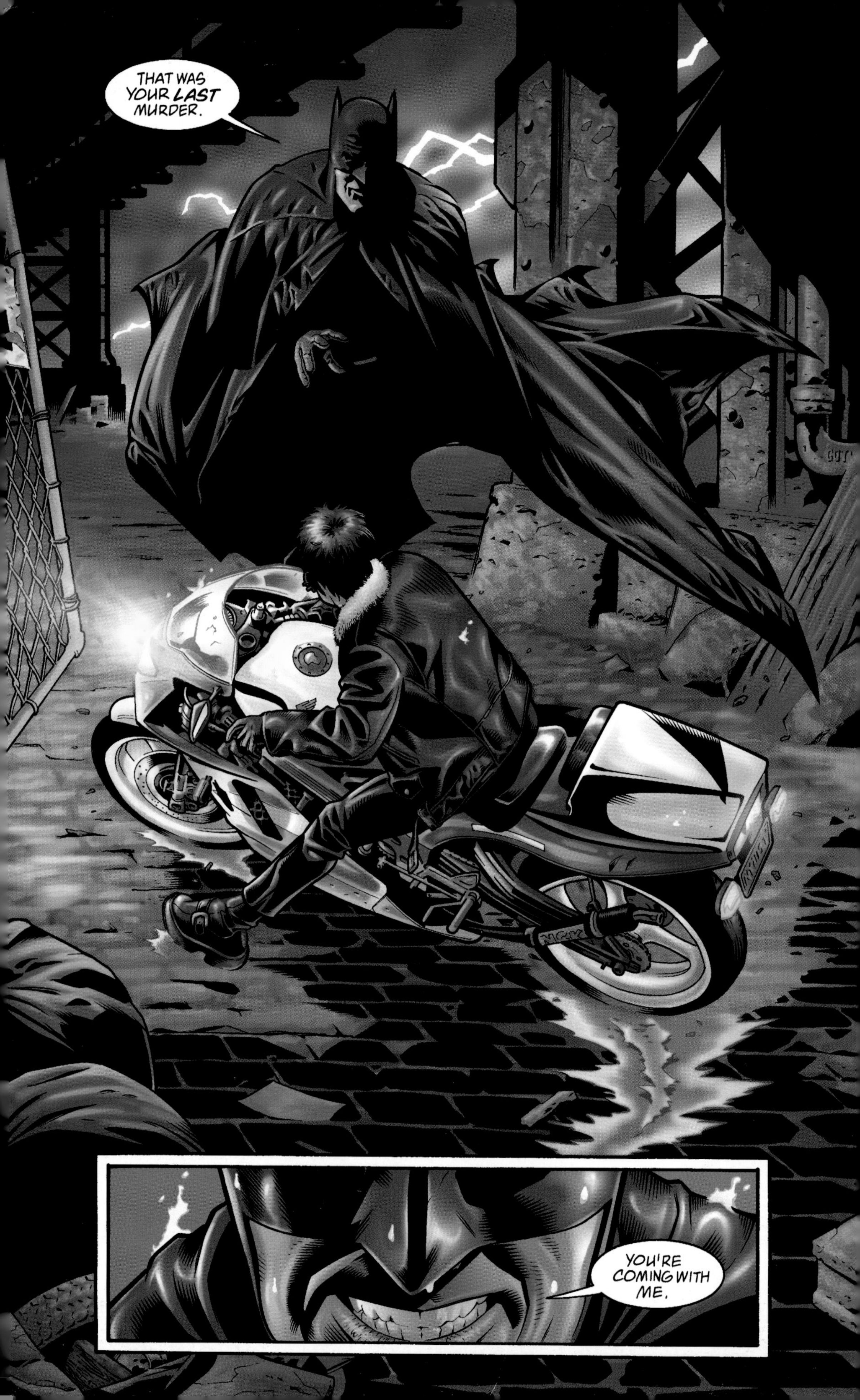
THAT WAS YOUR LAST MURDER.
YOU'RE COMING WITH ME.

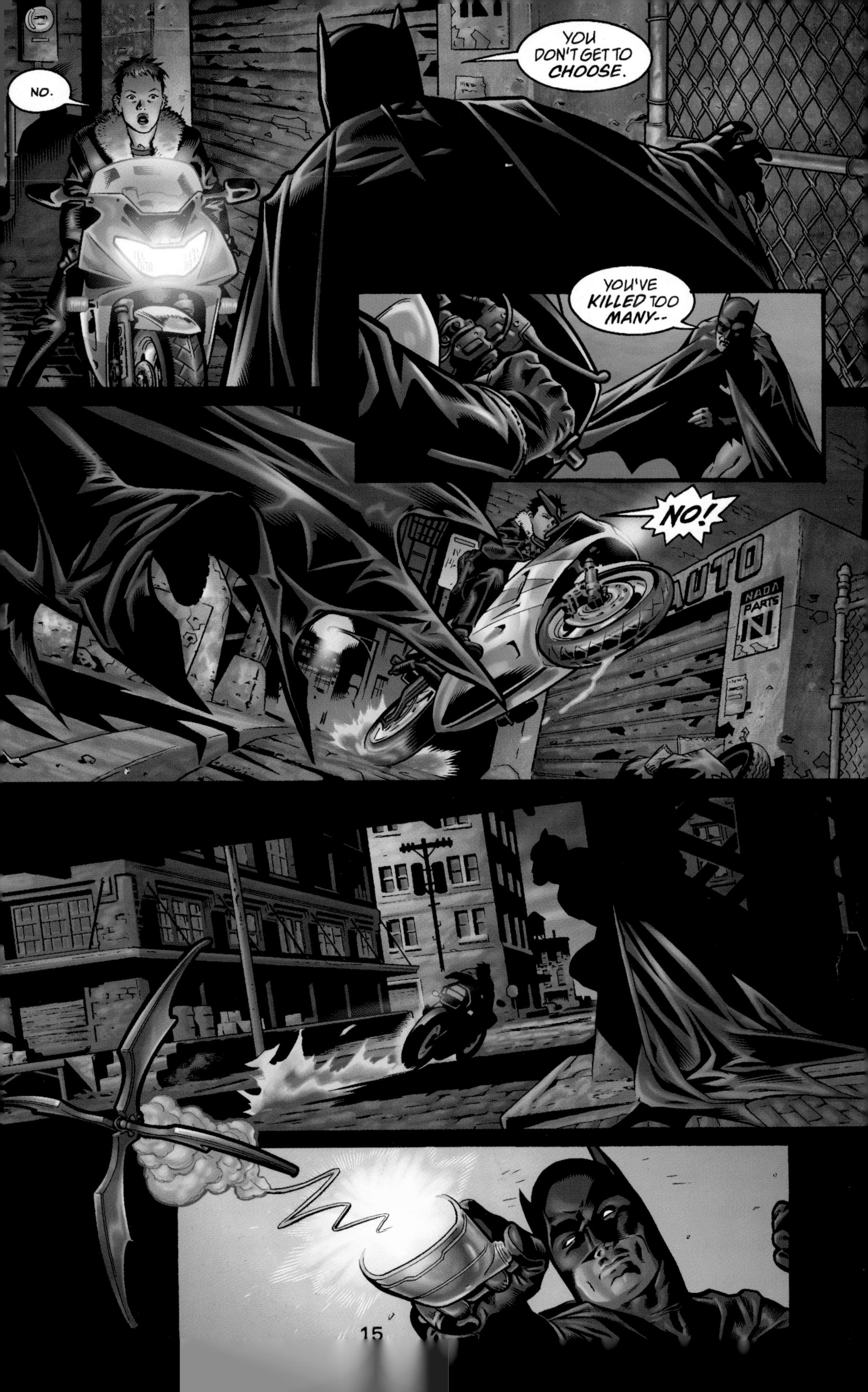
NO.
YOU DON'T GET TO CHOOSE.
YOU'VE KILLED TOO MANY--
NO!
AUTO
NADA PARTS

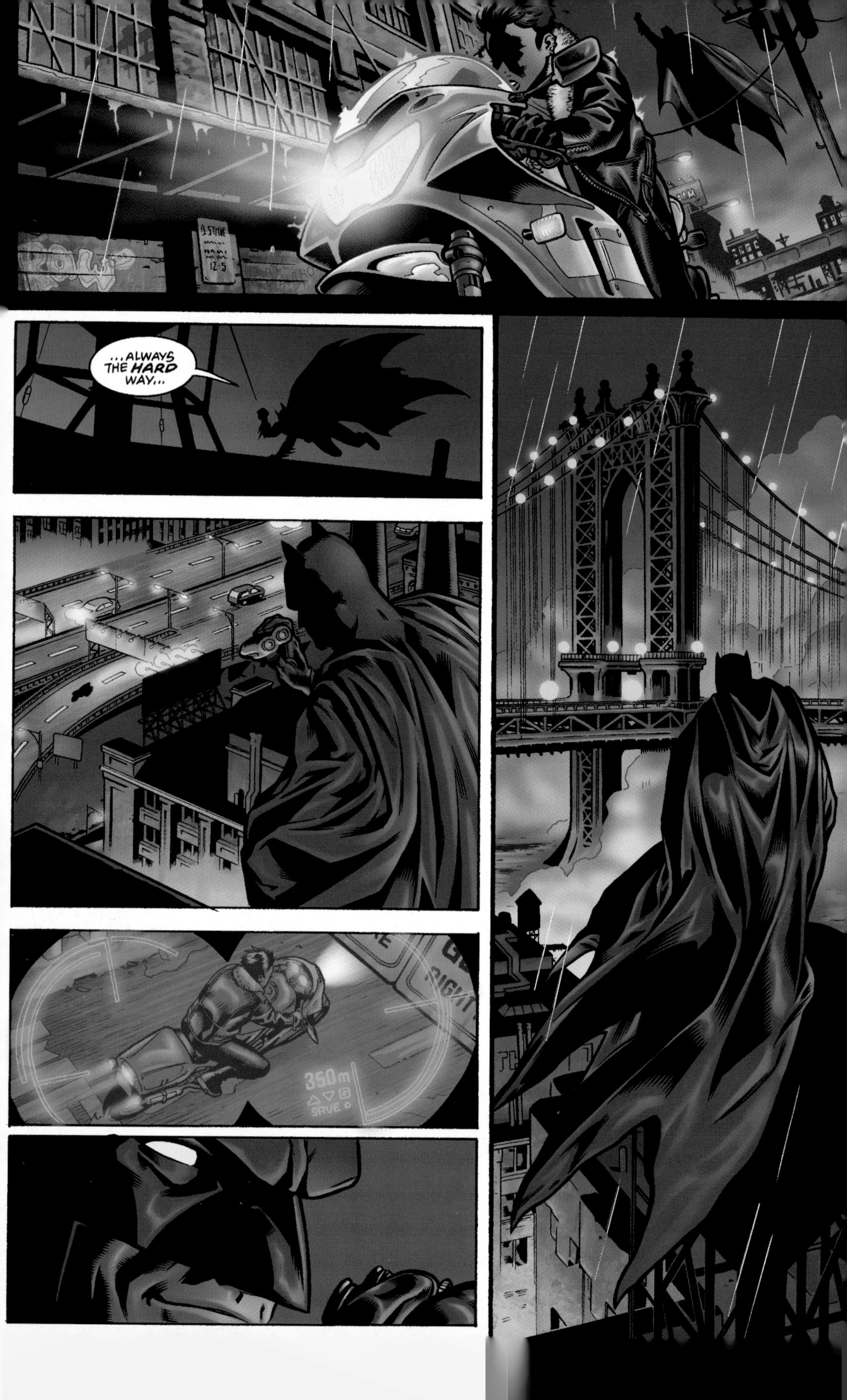
...ALWAYS THE HARD WAY...
350m

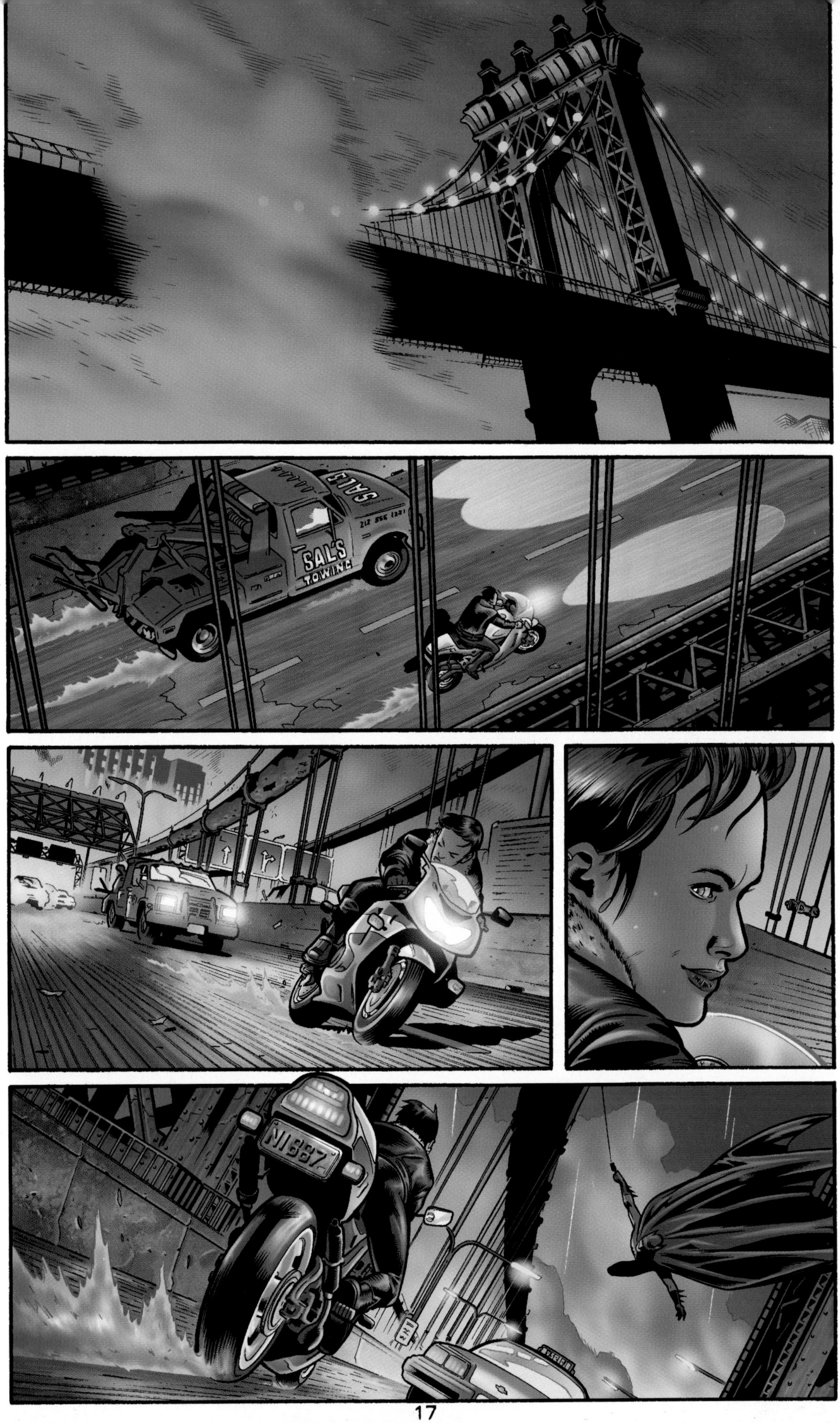
SALS
212 555 1231
SAL'S
TOWING
NI887

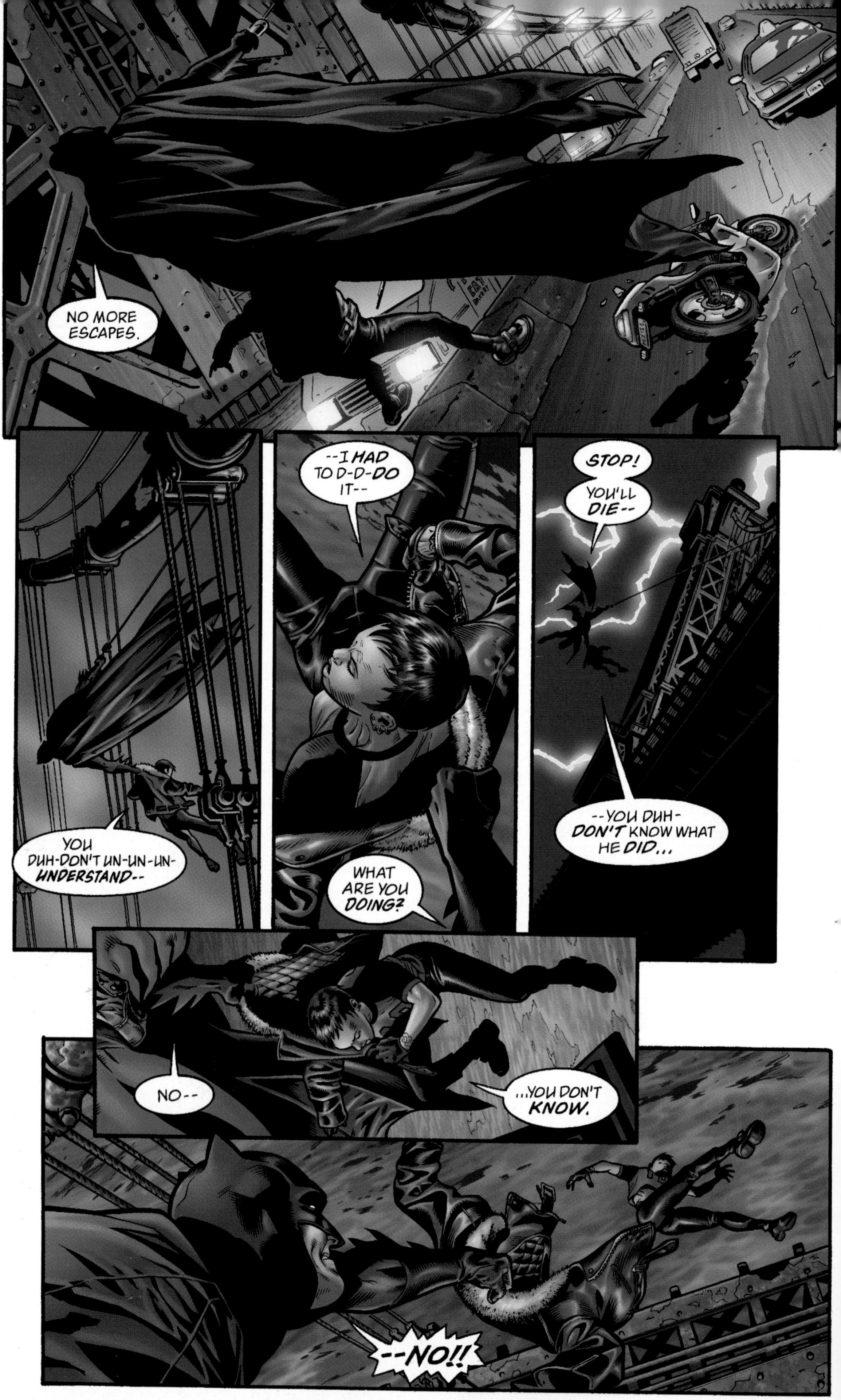

NO MORE ESCAPES.
YOU DUH-DON'T UN-UN-UN-UNDERSTAND--
--I HAD TO D-D-DO IT--
WHAT ARE YOU DOING?
STOP!
YOU'LL DIE--
--YOU DUH-DON'T KNOW WHAT HE DID...
NO--
...YOU DON'T KNOW.
--NO!!

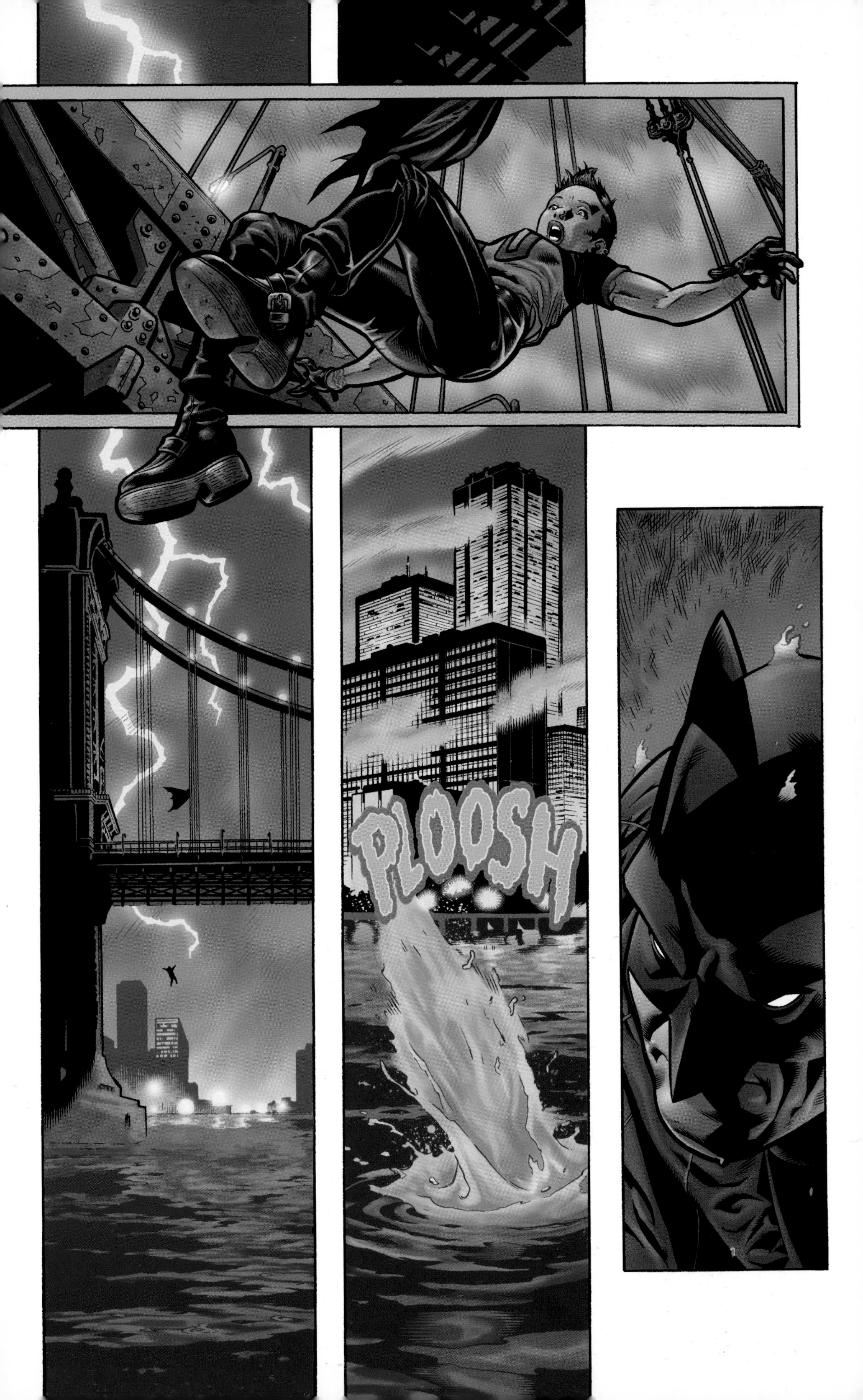
PLOOSH

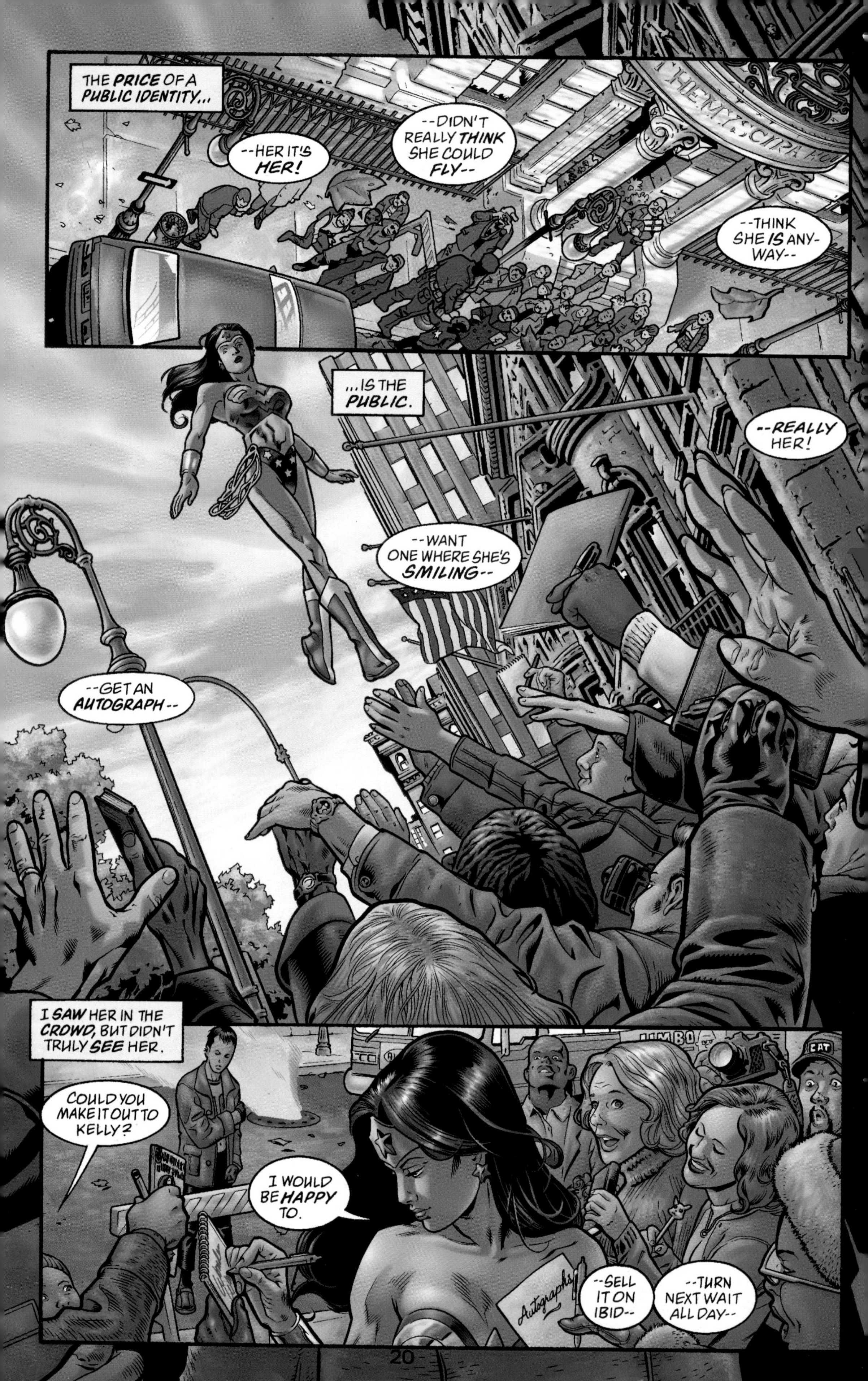
THE PRICE OF A PUBLIC IDENTITY...
--HER IT'S HER!
--DIDN'T REALLY THINK SHE COULD FLY--
--THINK SHE IS ANY-WAY--
...IS THE PUBLIC.
--REALLY HER!
--WANT ONE WHERE SHE'S SMILING--
--GET AN AUTOGRAPH--
I SAW HER IN THE CROWD, BUT DIDN'T TRULY SEE HER.
COULD YOU MAKE IT OUT TO KELLY?
I WOULD BE HAPPY TO.
--SELL IT ON IBID--
--TURN NEXT WAIT ALL DAY--

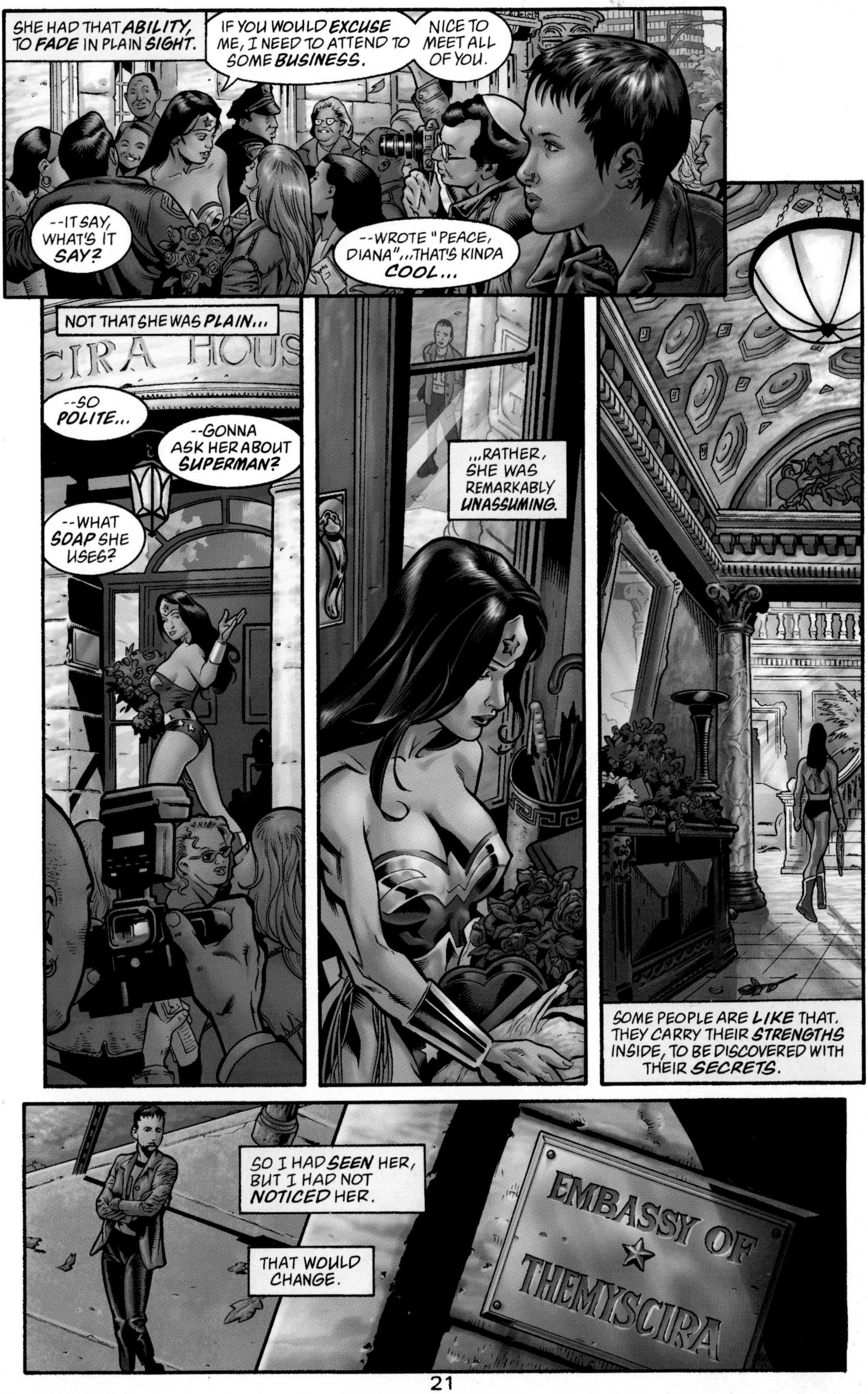

SHE HAD THAT ABILITY, TO FADE IN PLAIN SIGHT.
IF YOU WOULD EXCUSE ME, I NEED TO ATTEND TO SOME BUSINESS.
NICE TO MEET ALL OF YOU.
--IT SAY, WHAT'S IT SAY?
--WROTE "PEACE, DIANA"...THAT'S KINDA COOL...
NOT THAT SHE WAS PLAIN...
CIRA HOUS
--SO POLITE...
--GONNA ASK HER ABOUT SUPERMAN?
--WHAT SOAP SHE USES?
...RATHER, SHE WAS REMARKABLY UNASSUMING.
SOME PEOPLE ARE LIKE THAT. THEY CARRY THEIR STRENGTHS INSIDE, TO BE DISCOVERED WITH THEIR SECRETS.
SO I HAD SEEN HER, BUT I HAD NOT NOTICED HER.
THAT WOULD CHANGE.
EMBASSY OF THEMYSCIRA

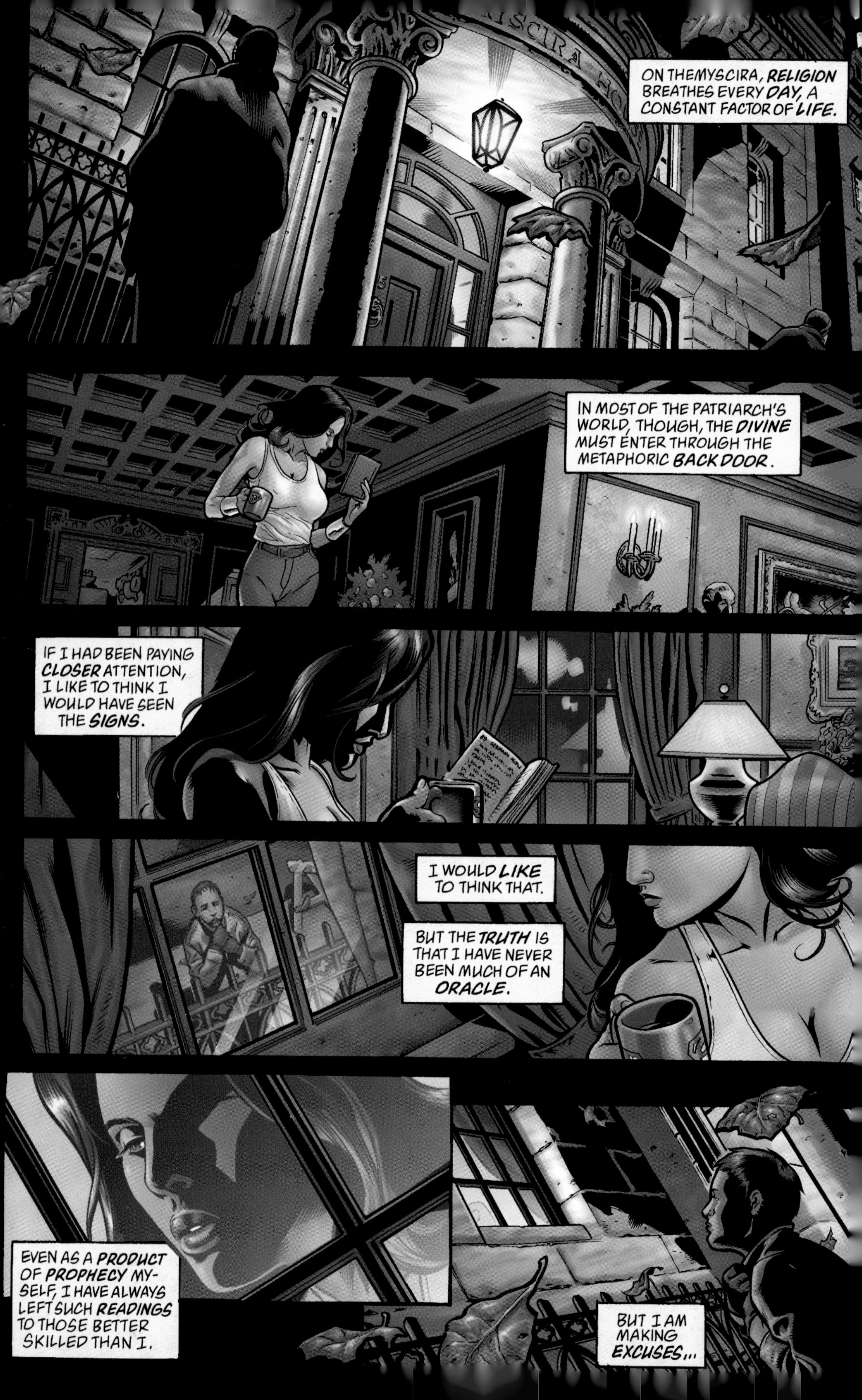

ON THEMYSCIRA, RELIGION BREATHES EVERY DAY, A CONSTANT FACTOR OF LIFE.
IN MOST OF THE PATRIARCH'S WORLD, THOUGH, THE DIVINE MUST ENTER THROUGH THE METAPHORIC BACK DOOR.
IF I HAD BEEN PAYING CLOSER ATTENTION, I LIKE TO THINK I WOULD HAVE SEEN THE SIGNS.
I WOULD LIKE TO THINK THAT.
BUT THE TRUTH IS THAT I HAVE NEVER BEEN MUCH OF AN ORACLE.
EVEN AS A PRODUCT OF PROPHECY MY-SELF, I HAVE ALWAYS LEFT SUCH READINGS TO THOSE BETTER SKILLED THAN I.
BUT I AM MAKING EXCUSES...

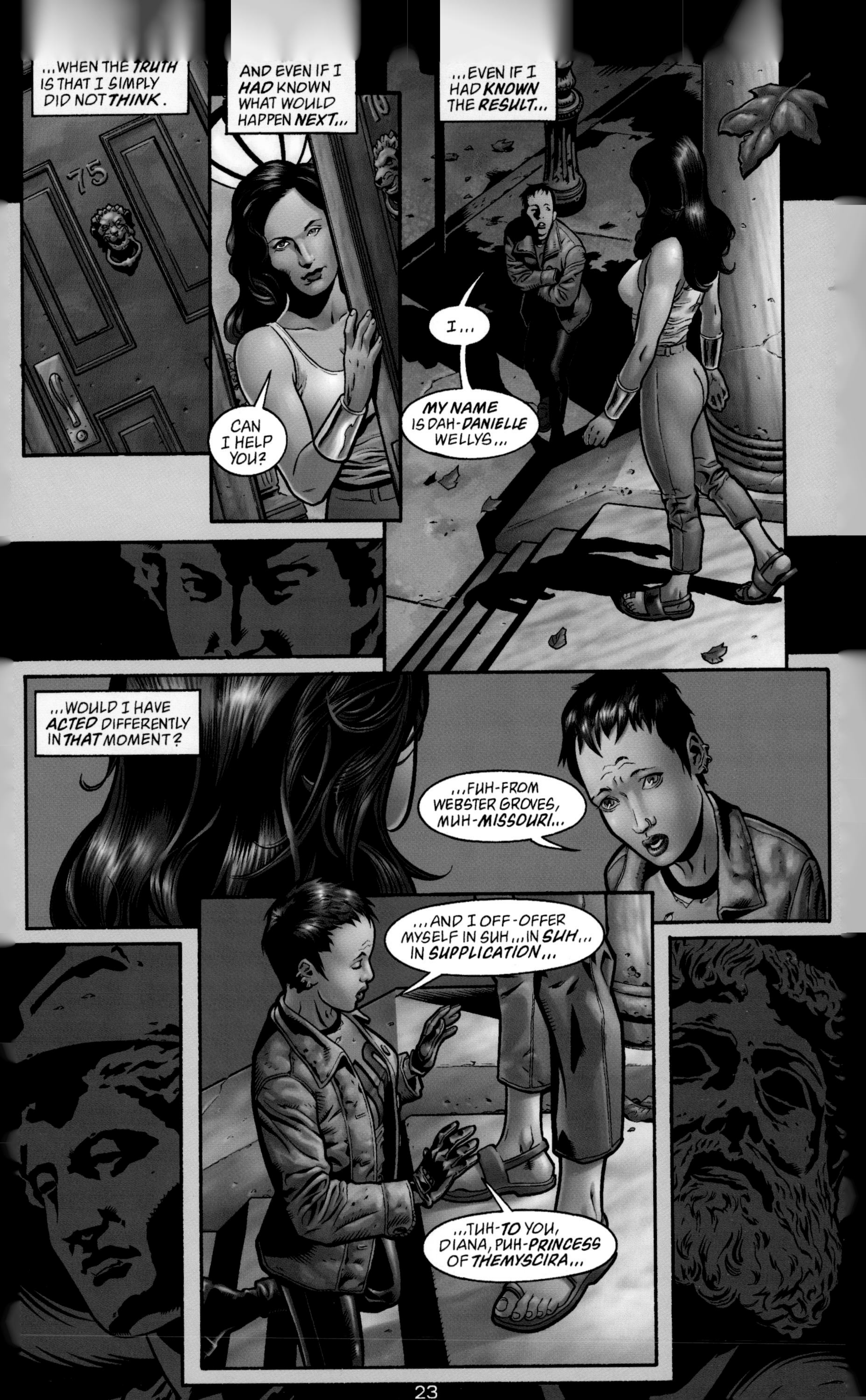
...WHEN THE TRUTH IS THAT I SIMPLY DID NOT THINK.
AND EVEN IF I HAD KNOWN WHAT WOULD HAPPEN NEXT...
CAN I HELP YOU?
...EVEN IF I HAD KNOWN THE RESULT...
I...
MY NAME IS DAH-DANIELLE WELLYS...
...WOULD I HAVE ACTED DIFFERENTLY IN THAT MOMENT?
...FUH-FROM WEBSTER GROVES, MUH-MISSOURI...
...AND I OFF-OFFER MYSELF IN SUH...IN SUH... IN SUPPLICATION...
...TUH-TO YOU, DIANA, PUH-PRINCESS OF THEMYSCIRA...

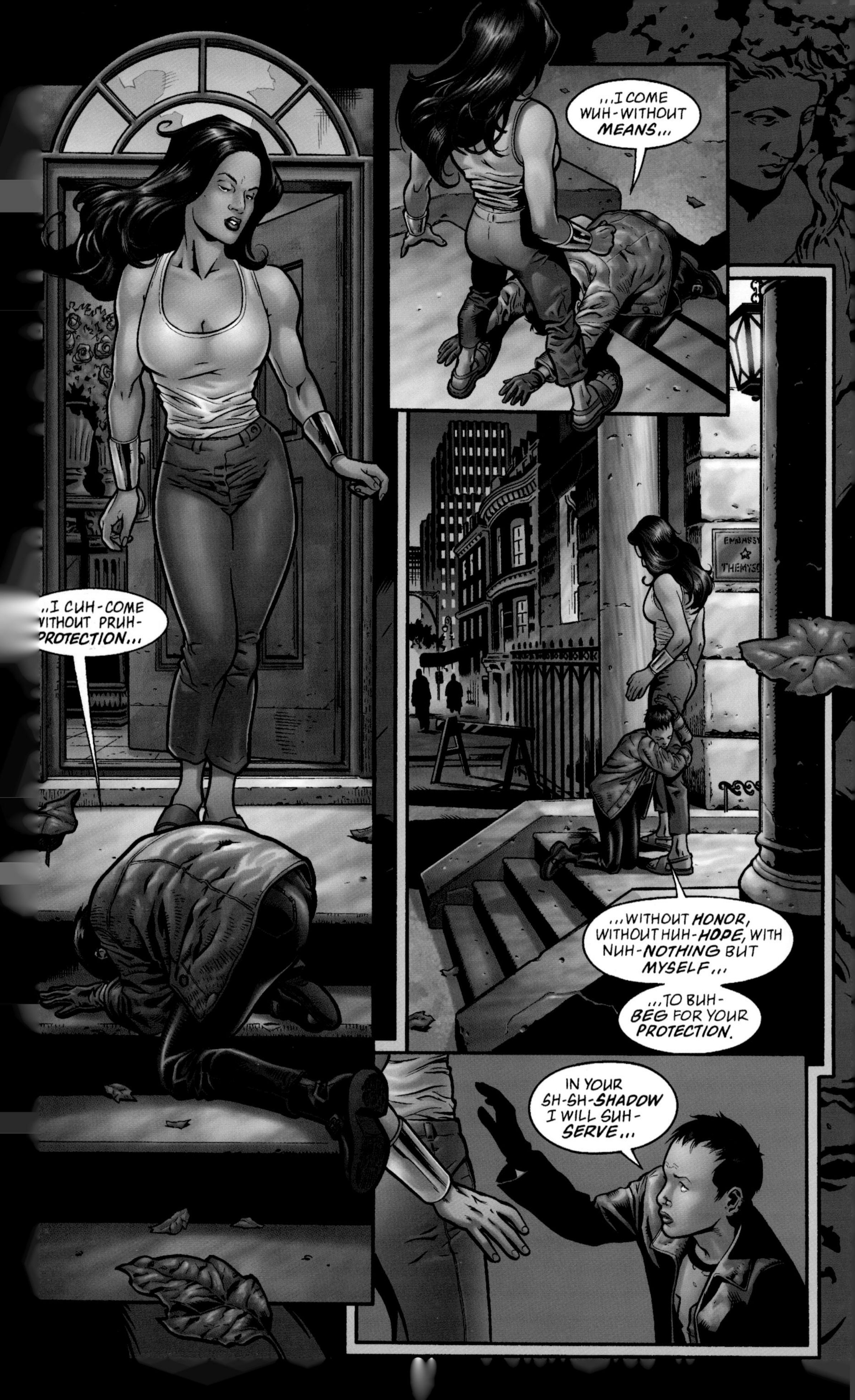
...I CUH-COME WITHOUT PRUH-PROTECTION...
...I COME WUH-WITHOUT MEANS...
EMBASSY THEMYS
...WITHOUT HONOR, WITHOUT HUH-HOPE, WITH NUH-NOTHING BUT MYSELF...
...TO BUH-BEG FOR YOUR PROTECTION.
IN YOUR SH-SH-SHADOW I WILL SUH-SERVE...

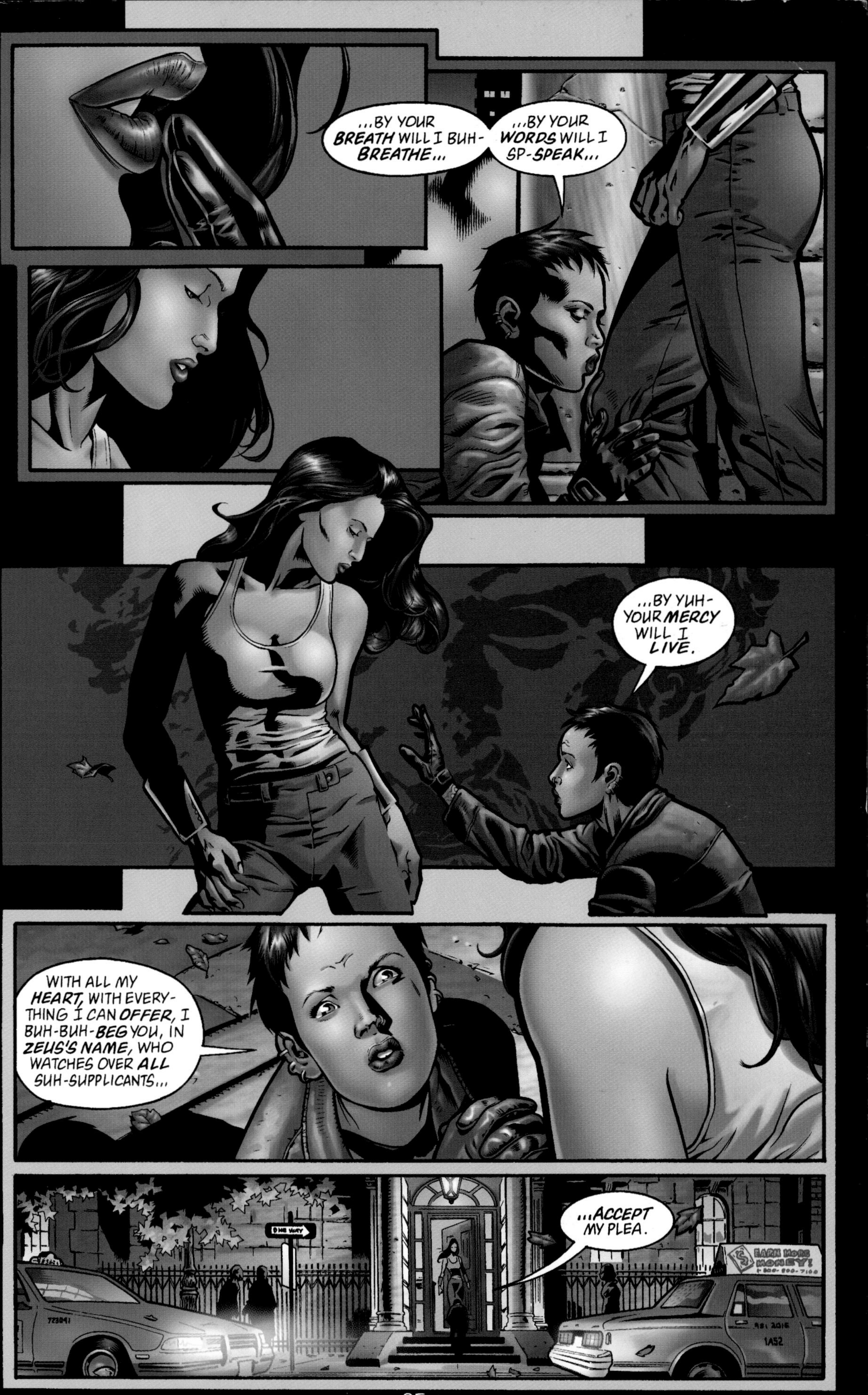
...BY YOUR BREATH WILL I BUH-BREATHE...
...BY YOUR WORDS WILL I SP-SPEAK...
...BY YUH-YOUR MERCY WILL I LIVE.
WITH ALL MY HEART, WITH EVERYTHING I CAN OFFER, I BUH-BUH-BEG YOU, IN ZEUS'S NAME, WHO WATCHES OVER ALL SUH-SUPPLICANTS...
...ACCEPT MY PLEA.
ONE WAY
EARN MORE MONEY!

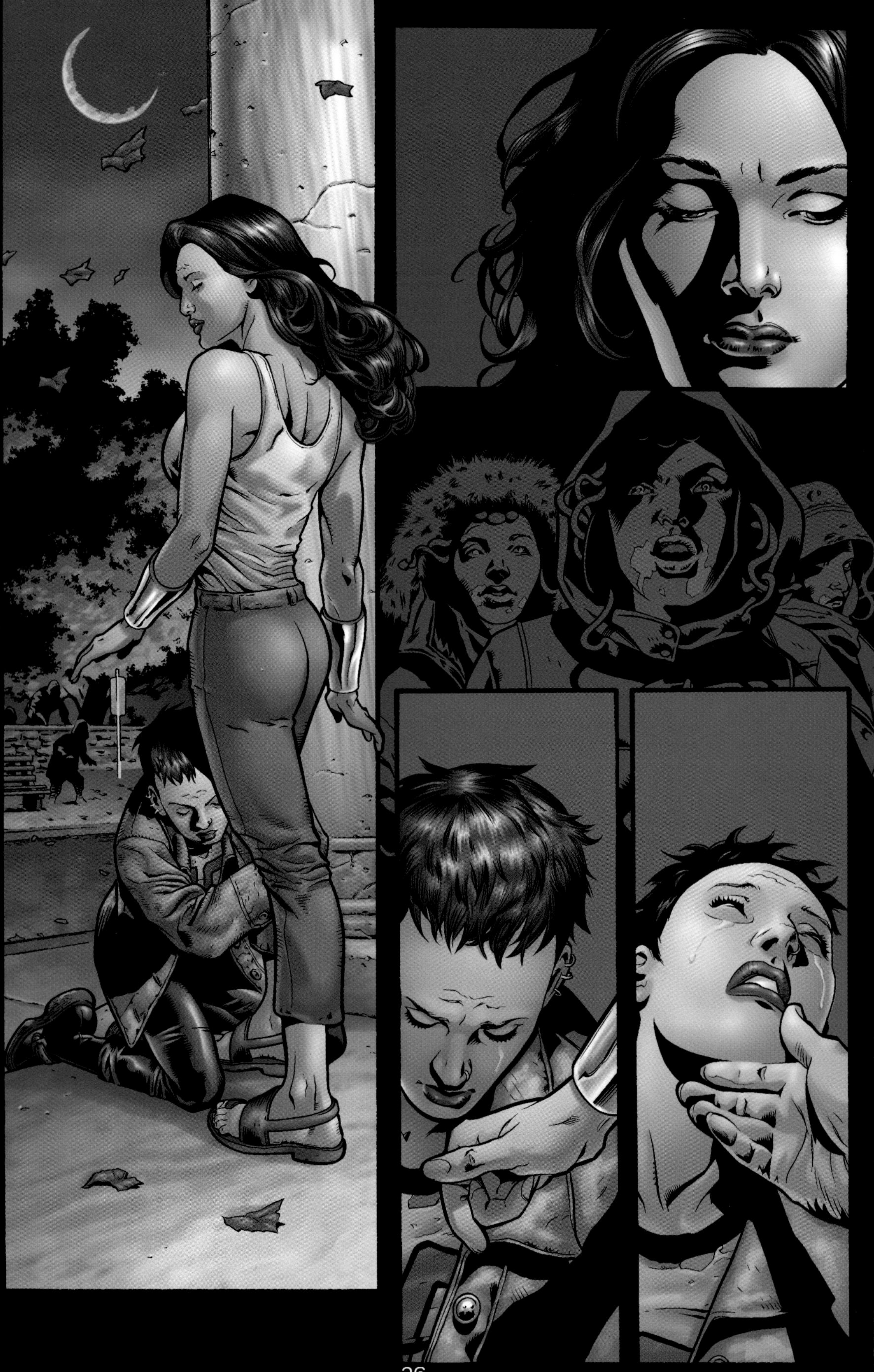

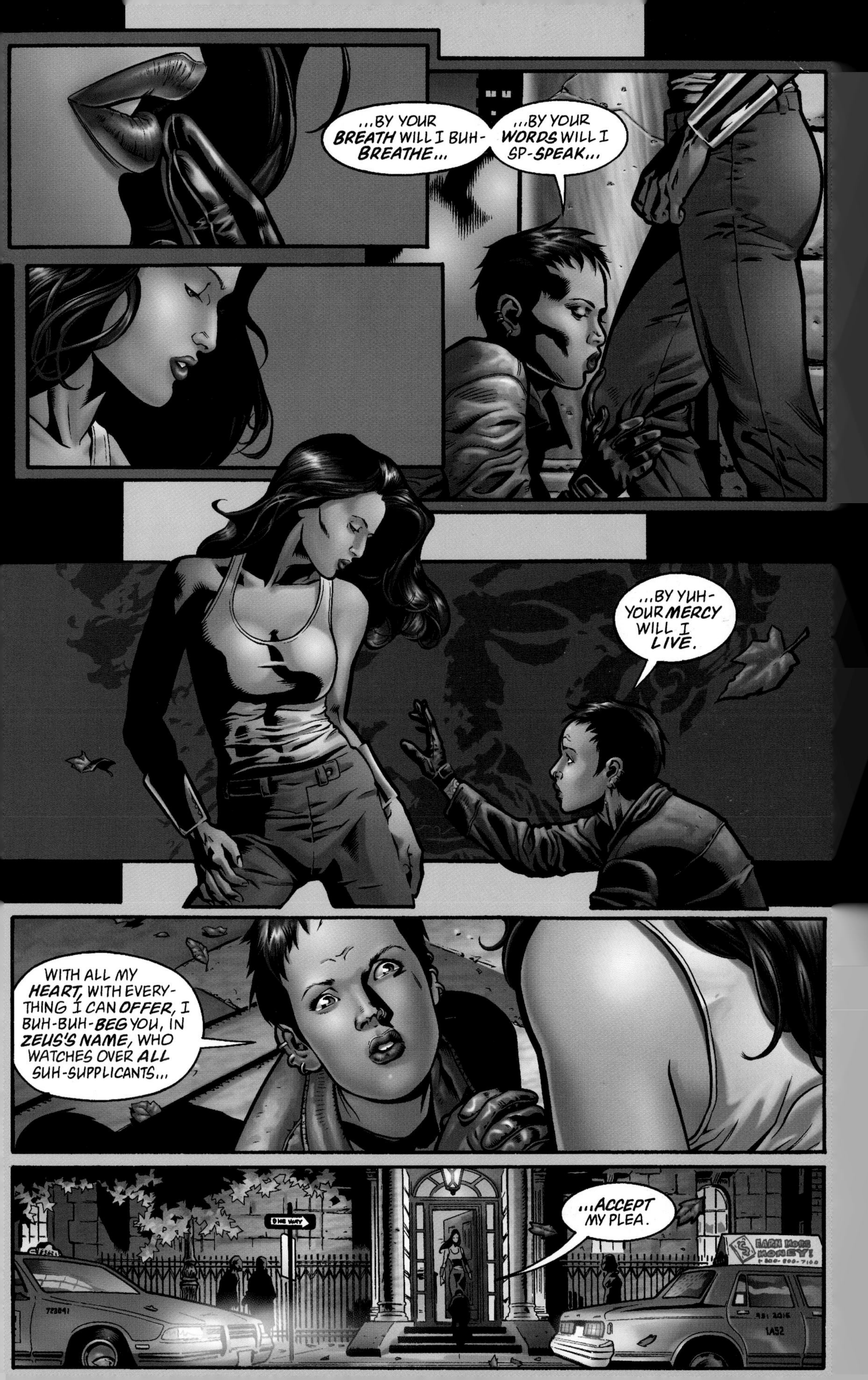
...BY YOUR BREATH WILL I BUH-BREATHE...
...BY YOUR WORDS WILL I SP-SPEAK...
...BY YUH-YOUR MERCY WILL I LIVE.
WITH ALL MY HEART, WITH EVERYTHING I CAN OFFER, I BUH-BUH-BEG YOU, IN ZEUS'S NAME, WHO WATCHES OVER ALL SUH-SUPPLICANTS...
...ACCEPT MY PLEA.
ONE WAY
EARN MORE MONEY!

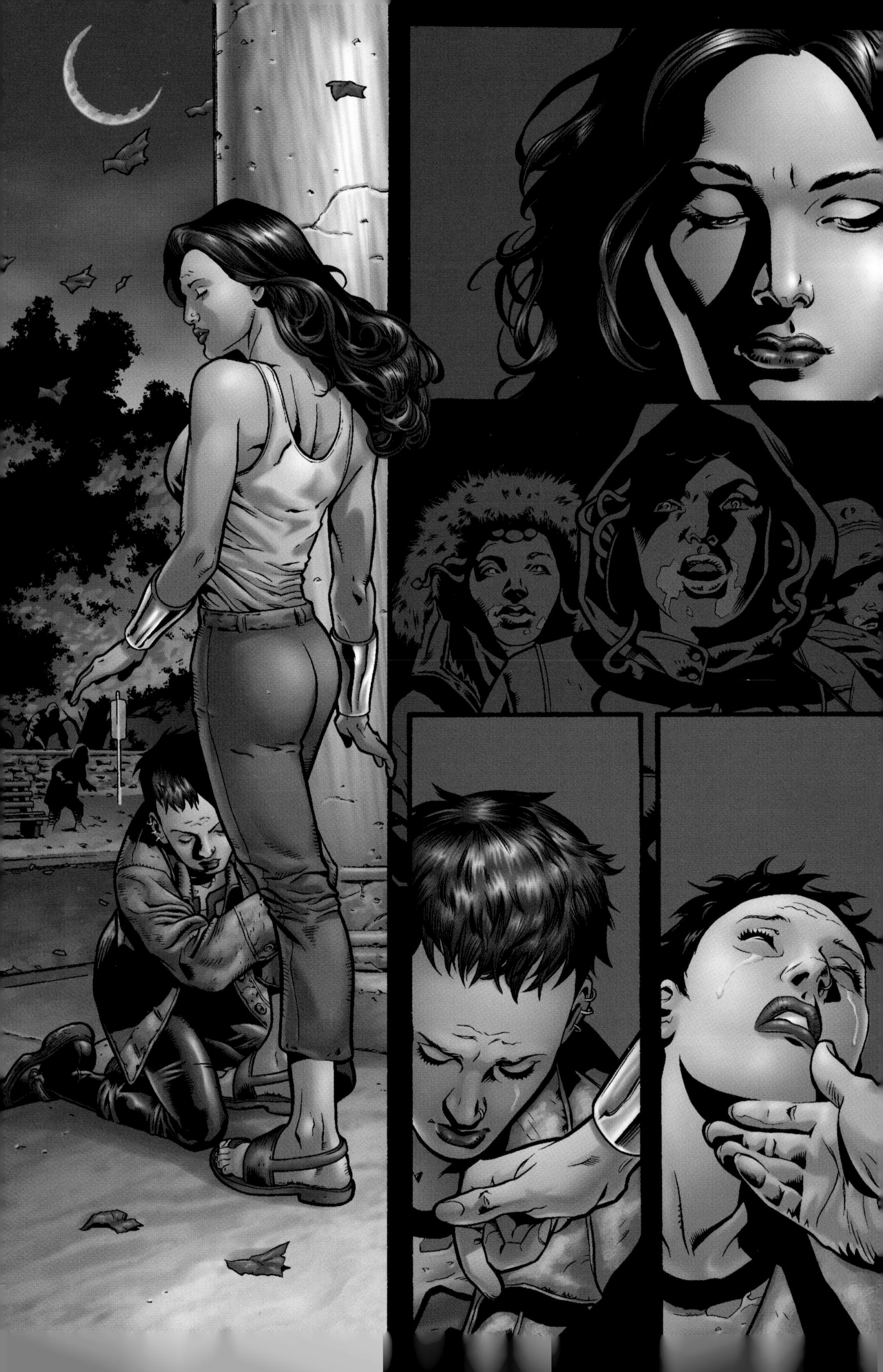

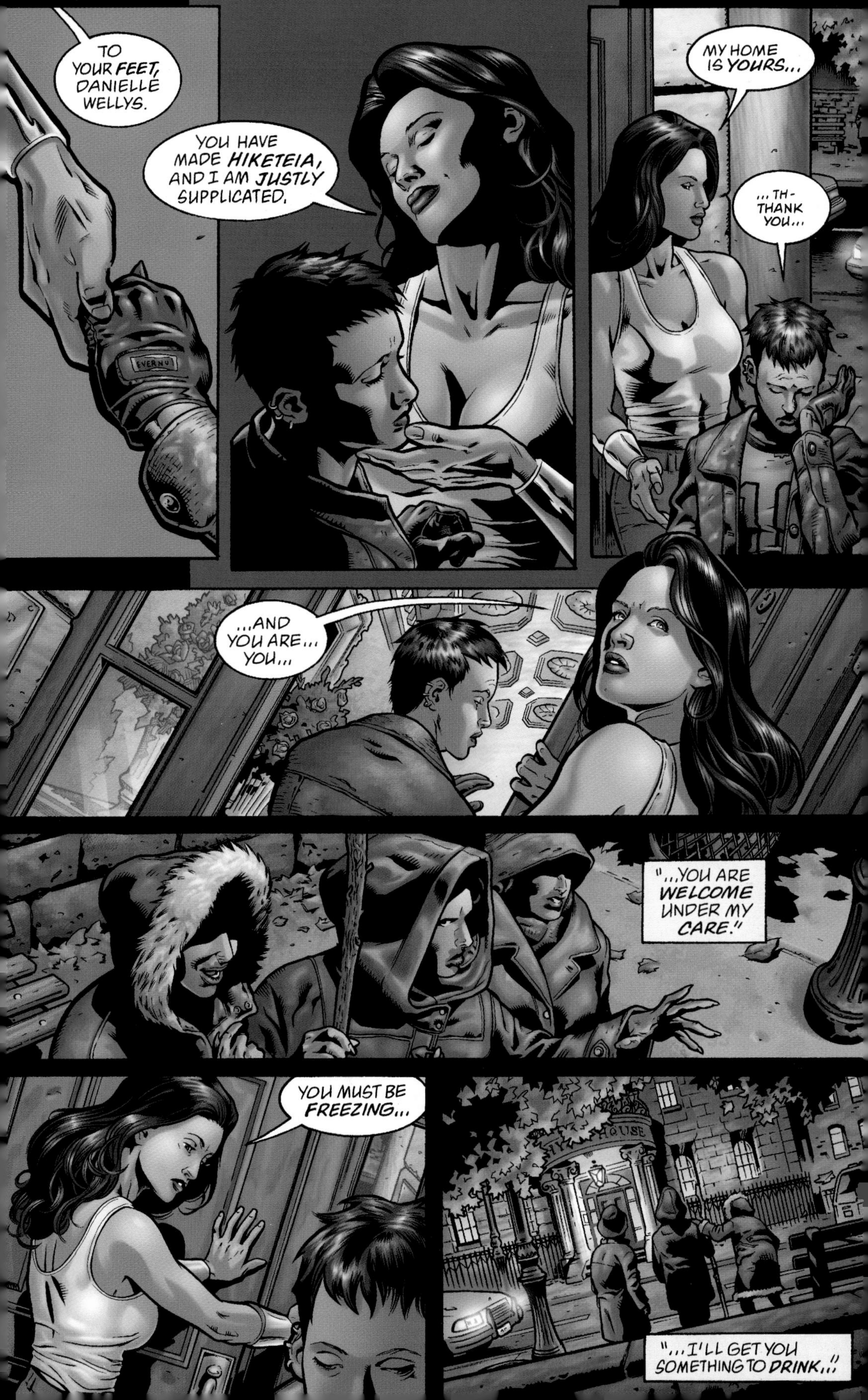
TO YOUR FEET, DANIELLE WELLYS.
YOU HAVE MADE HIKETEIA, AND I AM JUSTLY SUPPLICATED.
MY HOME IS YOURS...
...TH- THANK YOU...
...AND YOU ARE... YOU...
"...YOU ARE WELCOME UNDER MY CARE."
YOU MUST BE FREEZING...
"...I'LL GET YOU SOMETHING TO DRINK..."

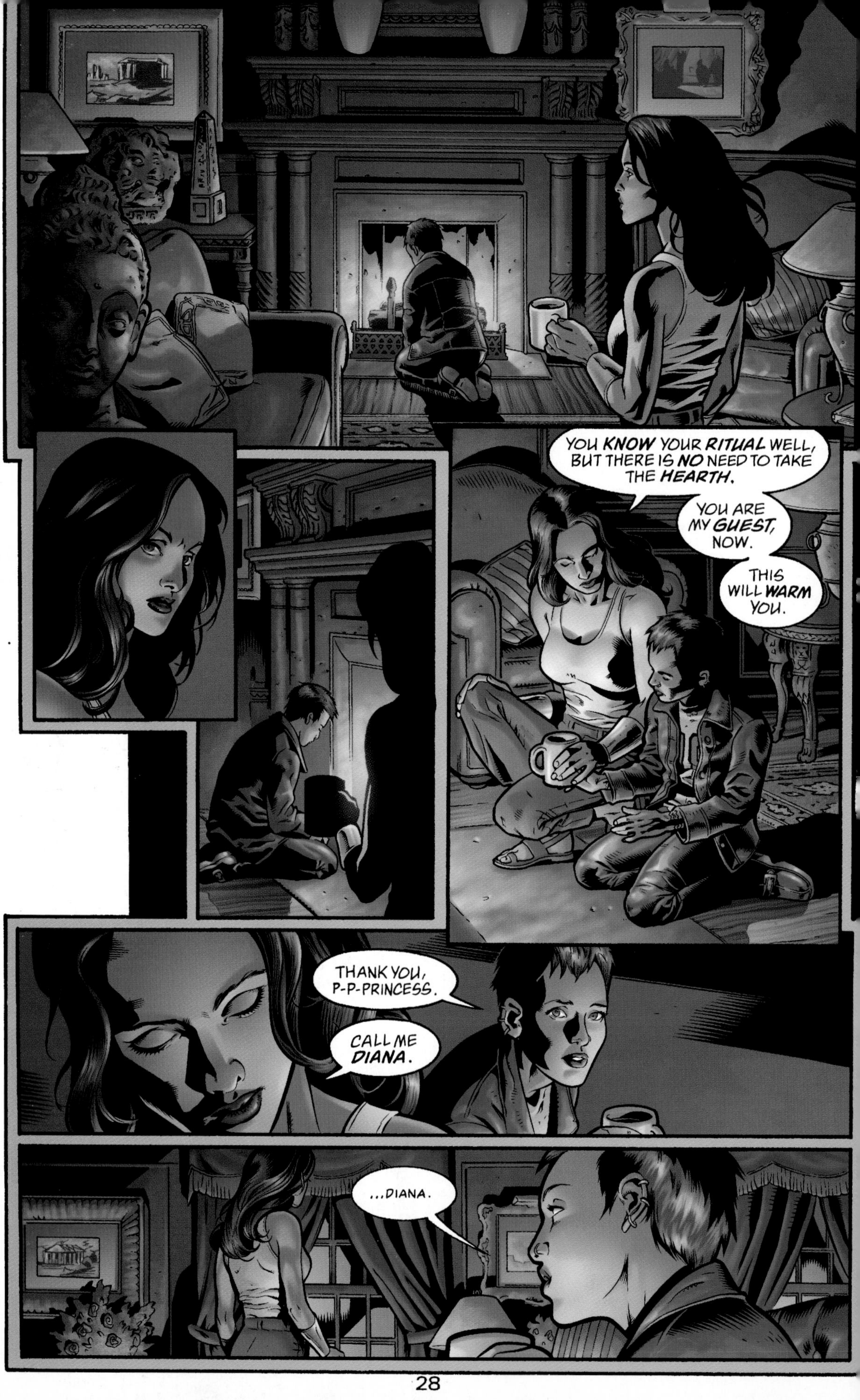
YOU KNOW YOUR RITUAL WELL, BUT THERE IS NO NEED TO TAKE THE HEARTH.
YOU ARE MY GUEST, NOW.
THIS WILL WARM YOU.
THANK YOU, P-P-PRINCESS.
CALL ME DIANA.
...DIANA.

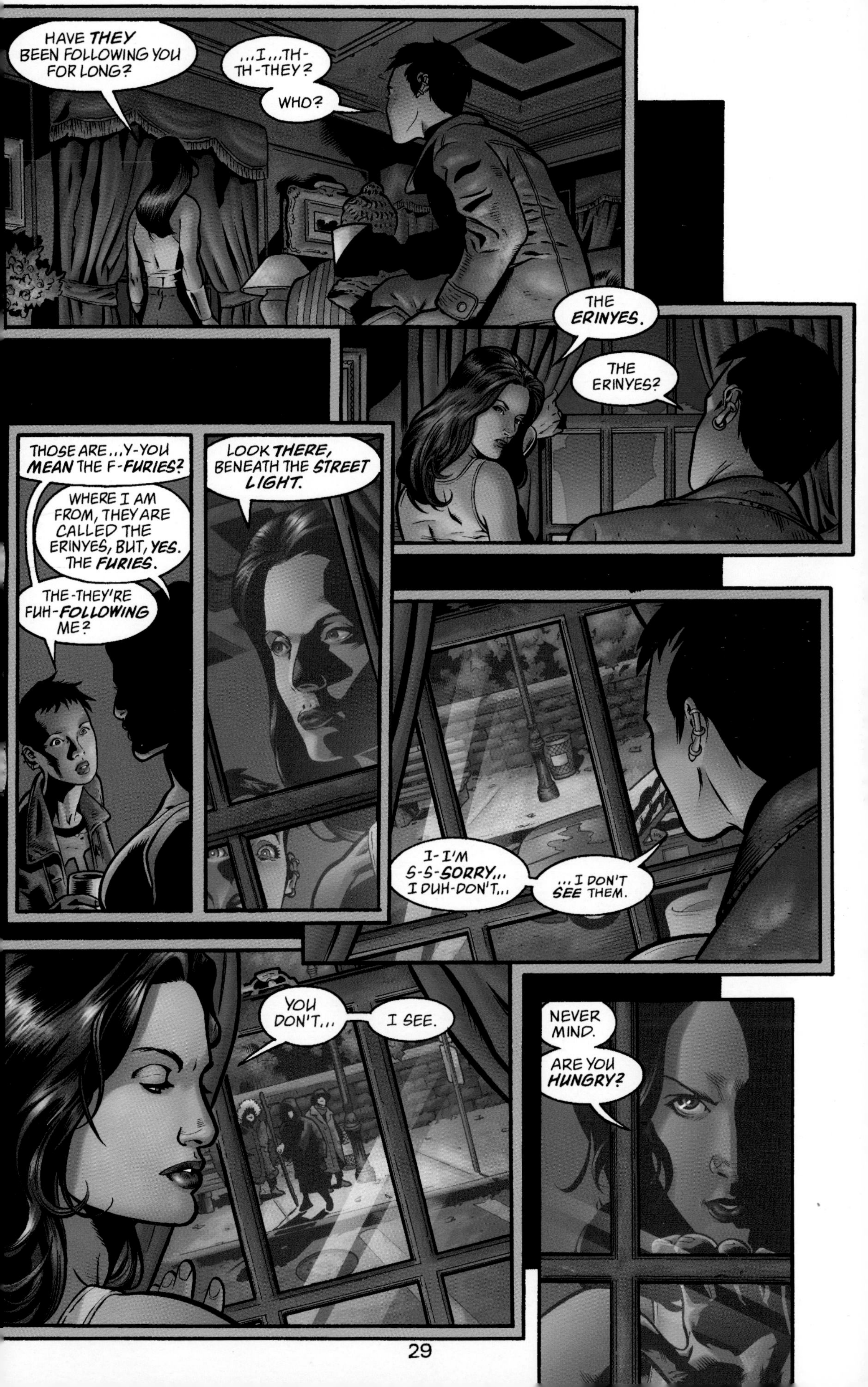
HAVE THEY BEEN FOLLOWING YOU FOR LONG?
...I...TH-TH-THEY?
WHO?
THE ERINYES.
THE ERINYES?
THOSE ARE...Y-YOU MEAN THE F-FURIES?
WHERE I AM FROM, THEY ARE CALLED THE ERINYES, BUT, YES. THE FURIES.
THE-THEY'RE FUH-FOLLOWING ME?
LOOK THERE, BENEATH THE STREET LIGHT.
I-I'M S-S-SORRY... I DUH-DON'T...
...I DON'T SEE THEM.
YOU DON'T...
I SEE.
NEVER MIND.
ARE YOU HUNGRY?

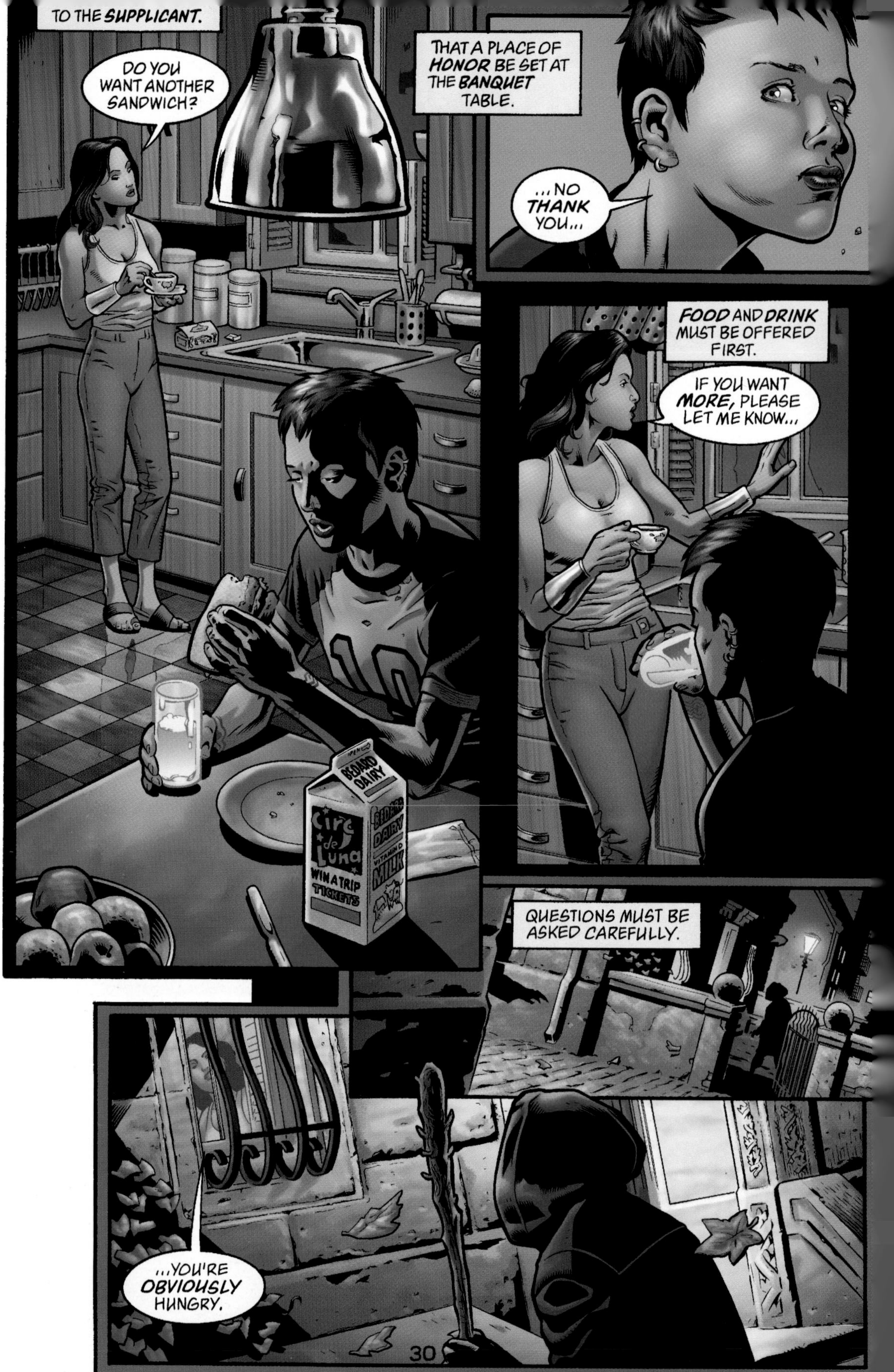
TO THE SUPPLICANT.
DO YOU WANT ANOTHER SANDWICH?
THAT A PLACE OF HONOR BE SET AT THE BANQUET TABLE.
...NO THANK YOU...
BEDARD DAIRY
Circ de Luna
WIN A TRIP
TICKETS
VITAMIN D MILK
FOOD AND DRINK MUST BE OFFERED FIRST.
IF YOU WANT MORE, PLEASE LET ME KNOW...
QUESTIONS MUST BE ASKED CAREFULLY.
...YOU'RE OBVIOUSLY HUNGRY.

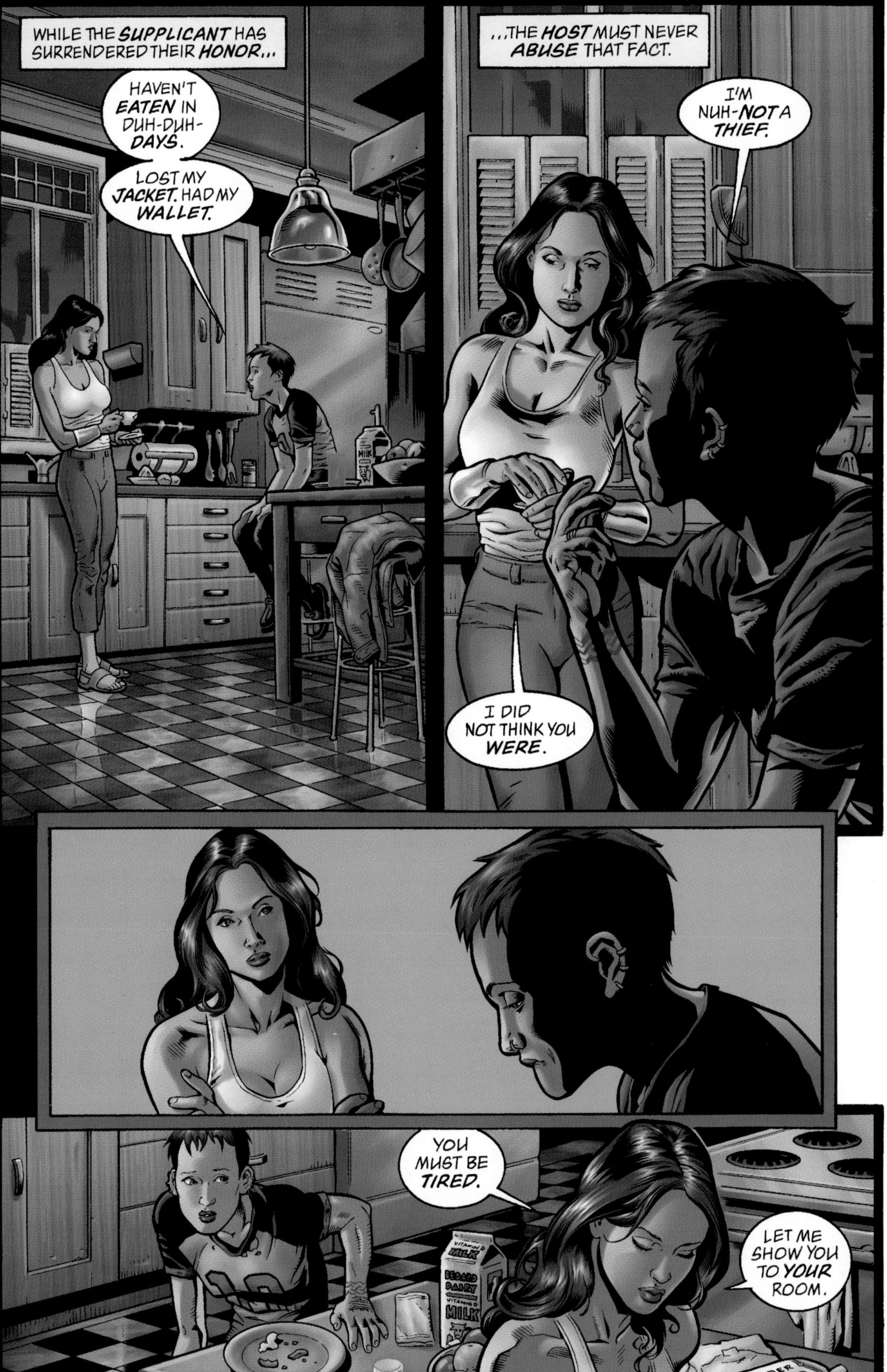
WHILE THE SUPPLICANT HAS SURRENDERED THEIR HONOR...
HAVEN'T EATEN IN DUH-DUH-DAYS.
LOST MY JACKET. HAD MY WALLET.
...THE HOST MUST NEVER ABUSE THAT FACT.
I'M NUH-NOT A THIEF.
I DID NOT THINK YOU WERE.
YOU MUST BE TIRED.
LET ME SHOW YOU TO YOUR ROOM.
VITAMIN D MILK
BEDARD DAIRY
WONDER LOAF

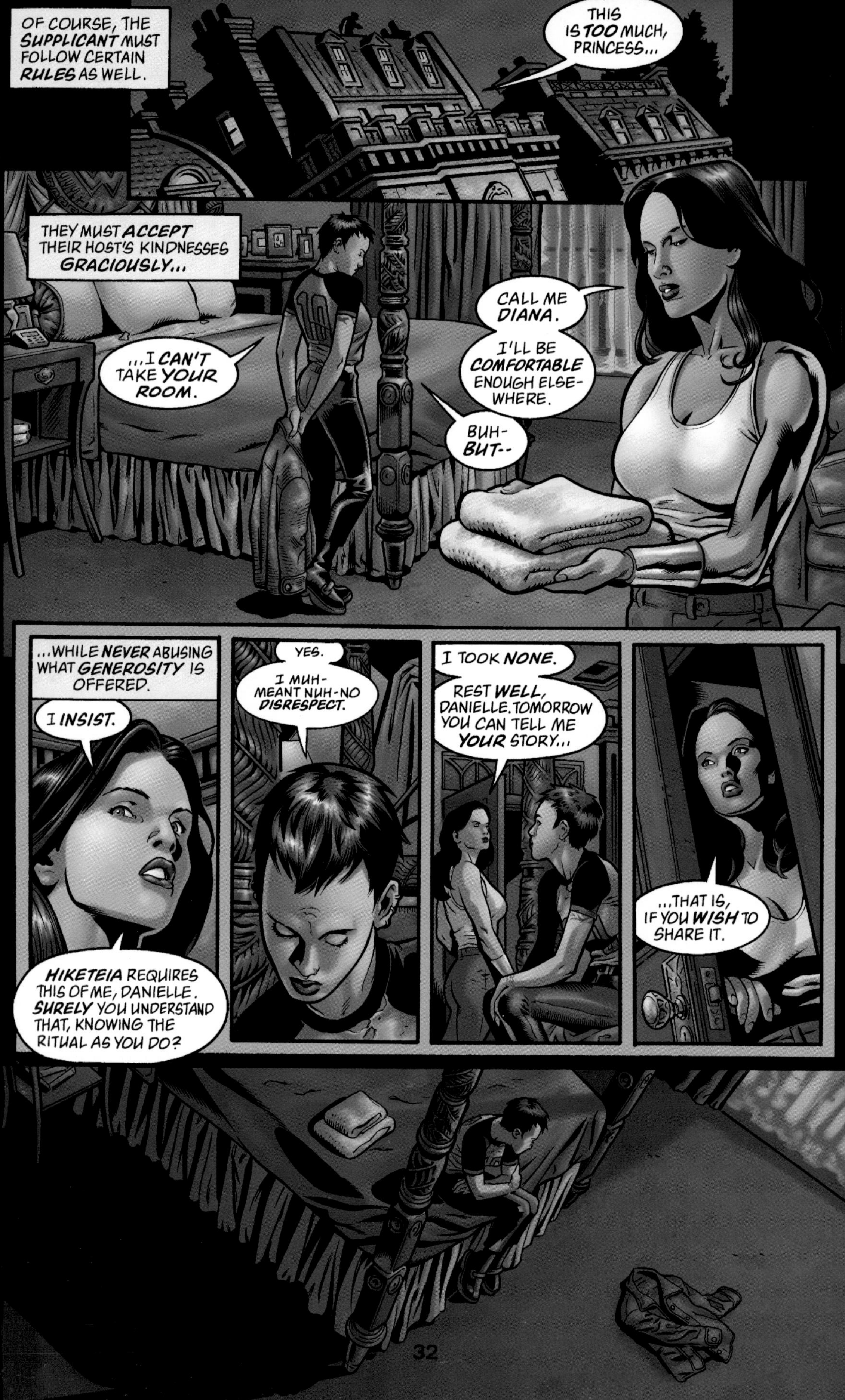

OF COURSE, THE SUPPLICANT MUST FOLLOW CERTAIN RULES AS WELL.
THIS IS TOO MUCH, PRINCESS...
THEY MUST ACCEPT THEIR HOST'S KINDNESSES GRACIOUSLY...
...I CAN'T TAKE YOUR ROOM.
CALL ME DIANA.
I'LL BE COMFORTABLE ENOUGH ELSE-WHERE.
BUH-BUT--
...WHILE NEVER ABUSING WHAT GENEROSITY IS OFFERED.
I INSIST.
HIKETEIA REQUIRES THIS OF ME, DANIELLE. SURELY YOU UNDERSTAND THAT, KNOWING THE RITUAL AS YOU DO?
YES.
I MUH-MEANT NUH-NO DISRESPECT.
I TOOK NONE.
REST WELL, DANIELLE. TOMORROW YOU CAN TELL ME YOUR STORY...
...THAT IS, IF YOU WISH TO SHARE IT.

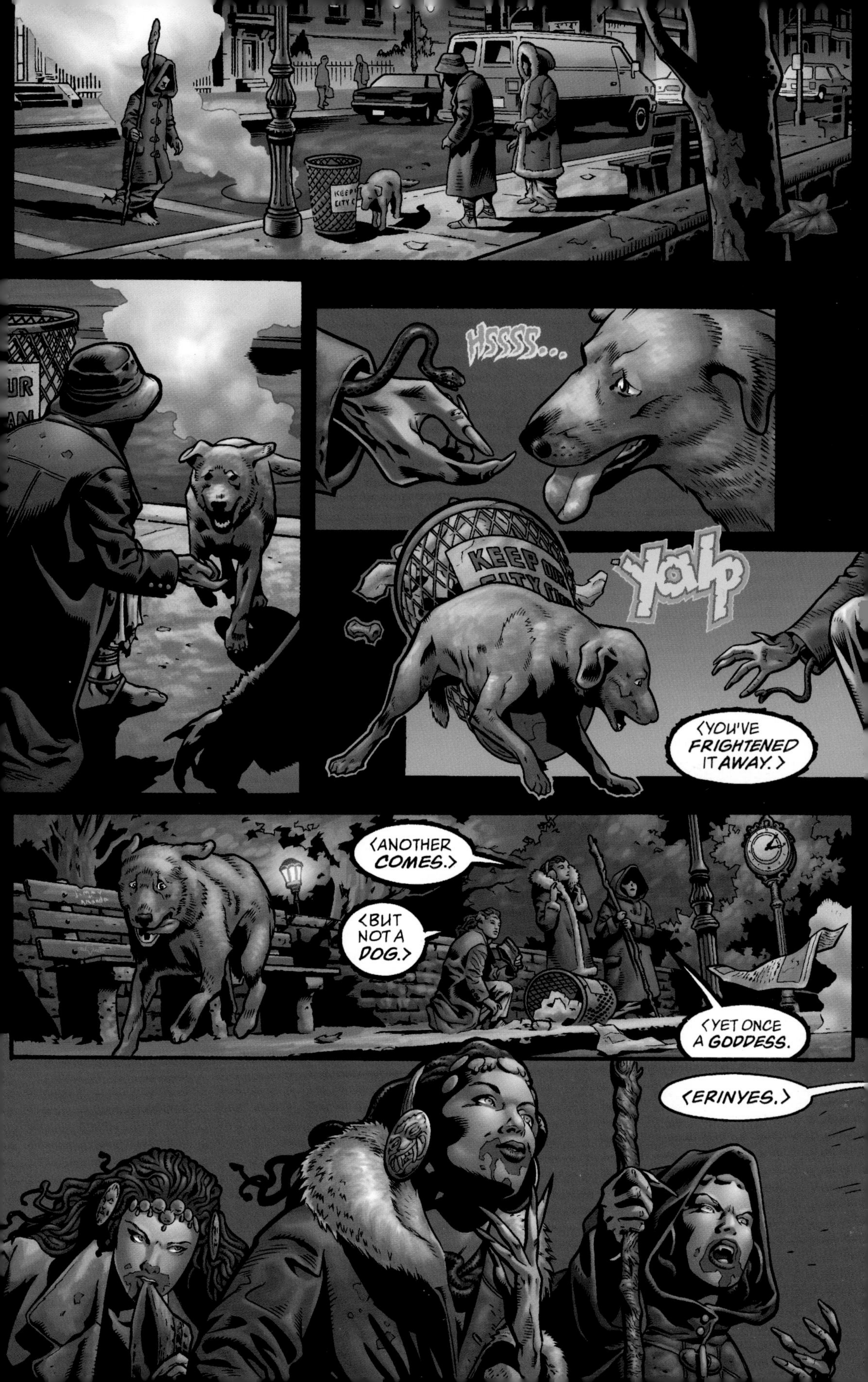
KEEP OUR CITY C
HSSSS...
KEEP OUR CITY CL
YALP
<YOU'VE FRIGHTENED IT AWAY.>
<ANOTHER COMES.>
<BUT NOT A DOG.>
<YET ONCE A GODDESS.
<ERINYES.>

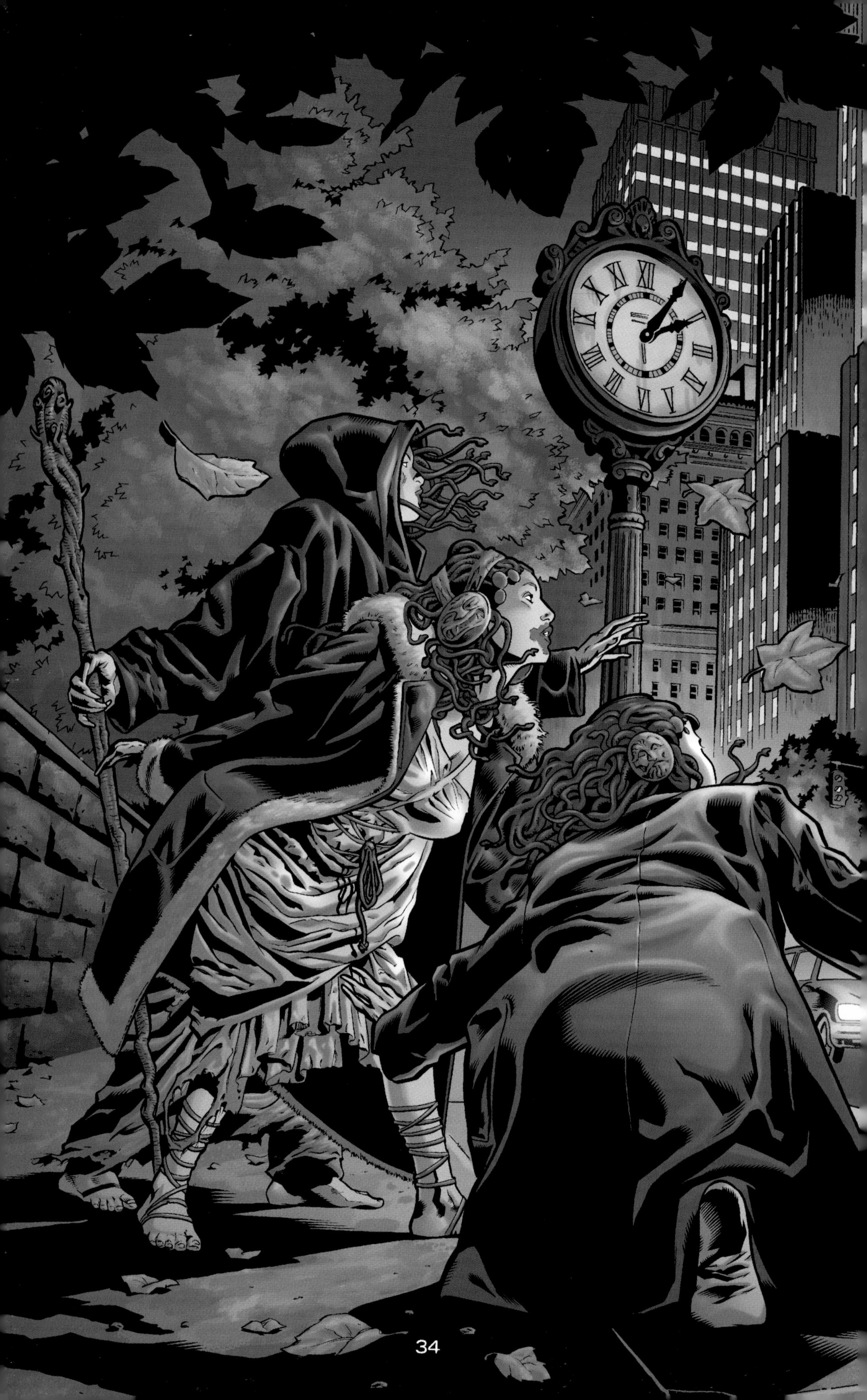

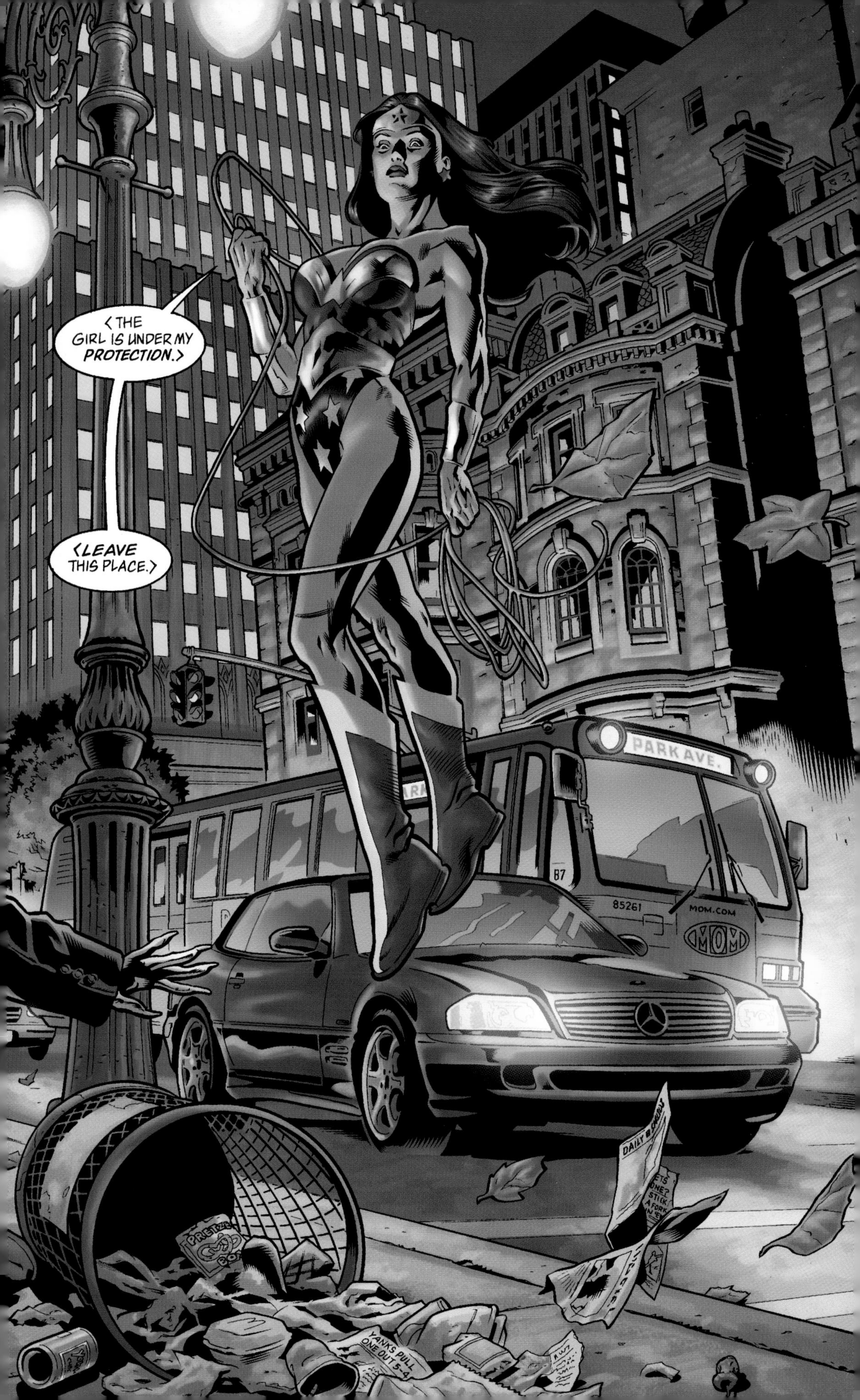
<THE GIRL IS UNDER MY PROTECTION.>
<LEAVE THIS PLACE.>
PARK AVE.
B7
85261
MOM.COM
MOM
YANKS PULL ONE OUT 5-4

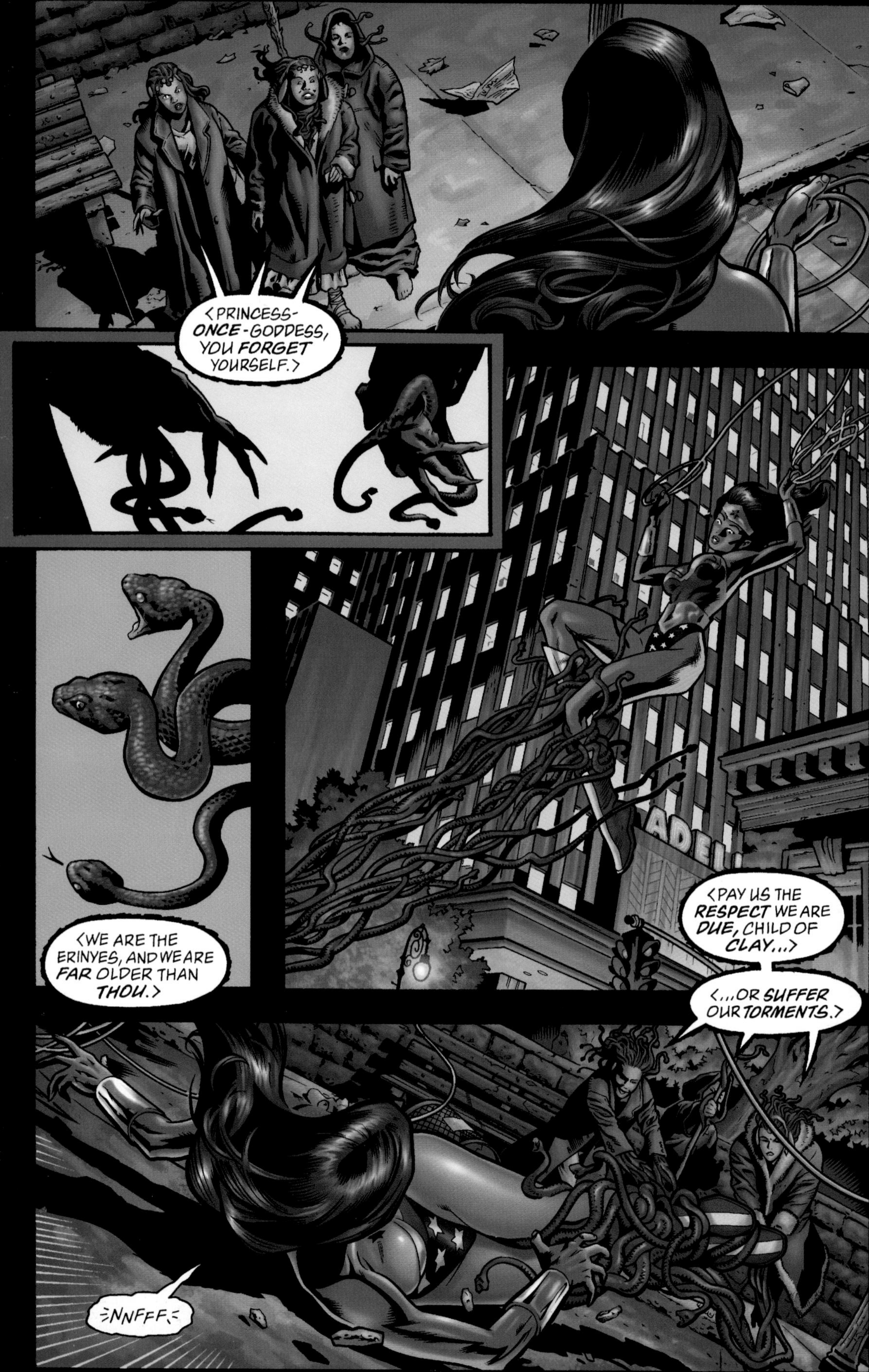

<PRINCESS-ONCE-GODDESS, YOU FORGET YOURSELF.>
<WE ARE THE ERINYES, AND WE ARE FAR OLDER THAN THOU.>
<PAY US THE RESPECT WE ARE DUE, CHILD OF CLAY...>
<...OR SUFFER OUR TORMENTS.>
NNFFF

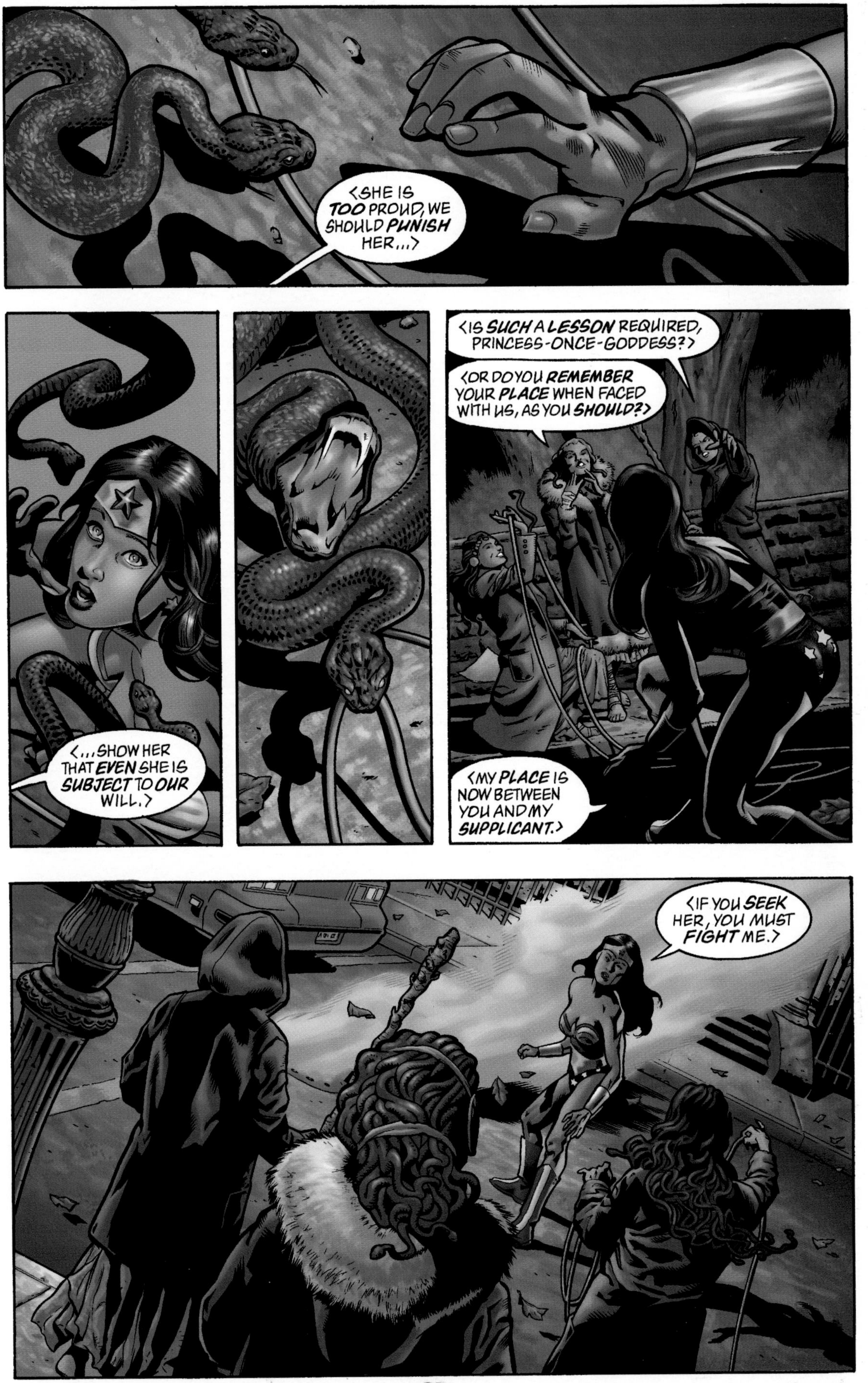
<SHE IS TOO PROUD, WE SHOULD PUNISH HER...>
<...SHOW HER THAT EVEN SHE IS SUBJECT TO OUR WILL.>
<IS SUCH A LESSON REQUIRED, PRINCESS-ONCE-GODDESS?>
<OR DO YOU REMEMBER YOUR PLACE WHEN FACED WITH US, AS YOU SHOULD?>
<MY PLACE IS NOW BETWEEN YOU AND MY SUPPLICANT.>
<IF YOU SEEK HER, YOU MUST FIGHT ME.>

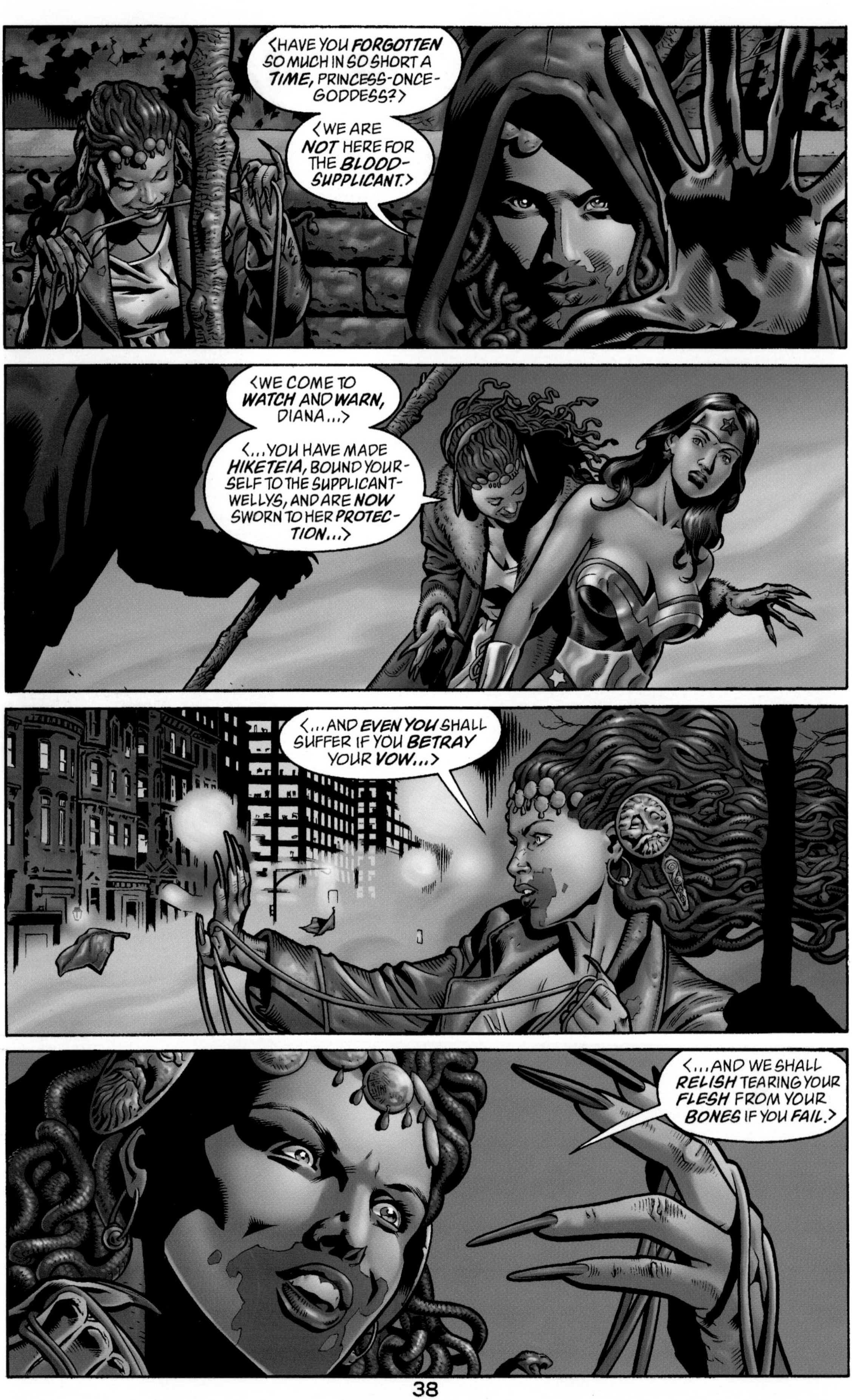

<HAVE YOU FORGOTTEN SO MUCH IN SO SHORT A TIME, PRINCESS-ONCE-GODDESS?>
<WE ARE NOT HERE FOR THE BLOOD-SUPPLICANT.>
<WE COME TO WATCH AND WARN, DIANA...>
<...YOU HAVE MADE HIKETEIA, BOUND YOURSELF TO THE SUPPLICANT-WELLYS, AND ARE NOW SWORN TO HER PROTECTION...>
<...AND EVEN YOU SHALL SUFFER IF YOU BETRAY YOUR VOW...>
<...AND WE SHALL RELISH TEARING YOUR FLESH FROM YOUR BONES IF YOU FAIL.>

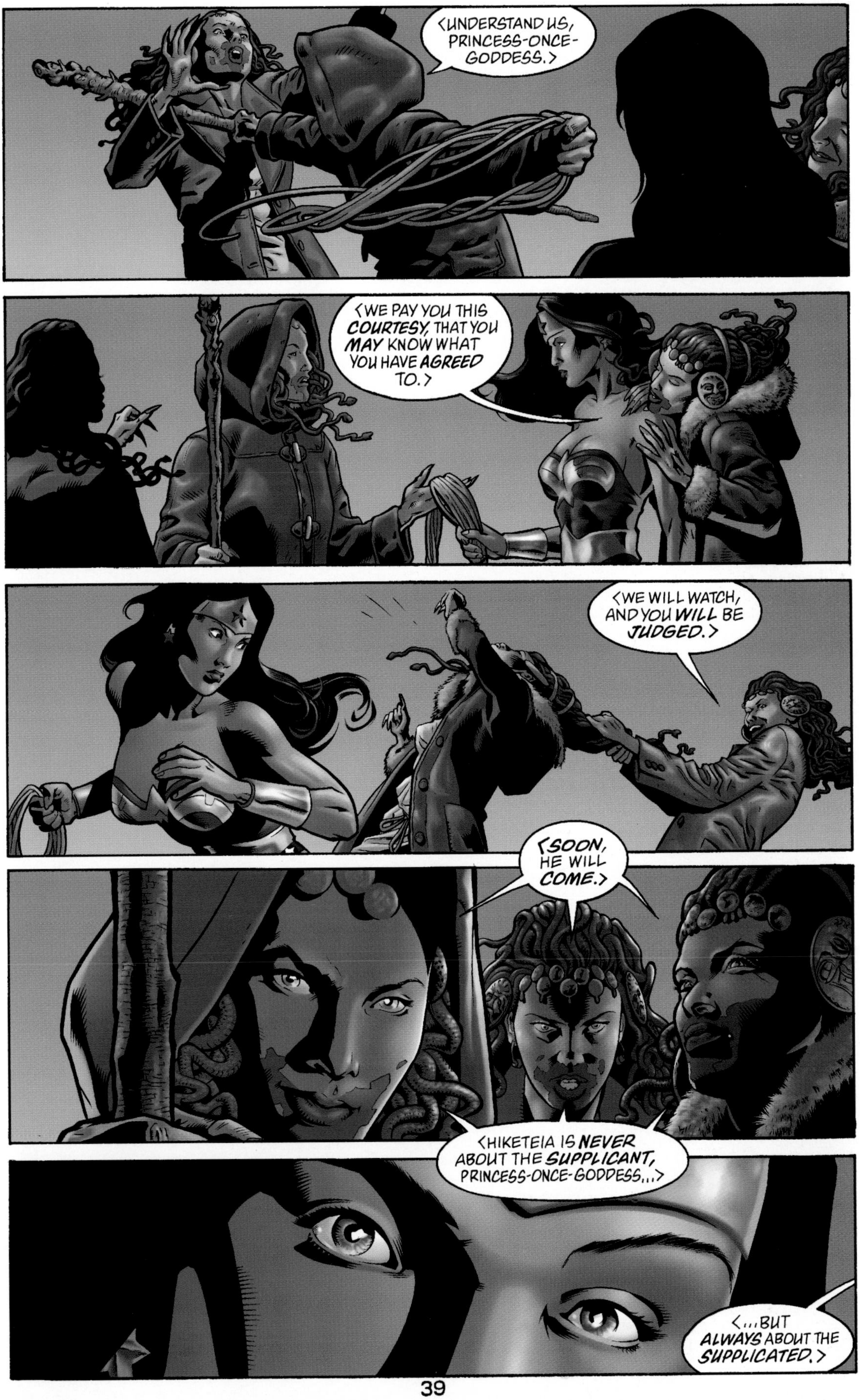
<UNDERSTAND US, PRINCESS-ONCE-GODDESS.>
<WE PAY YOU THIS COURTESY, THAT YOU MAY KNOW WHAT YOU HAVE AGREED TO.>
<WE WILL WATCH, AND YOU WILL BE JUDGED.>
<SOON, HE WILL COME.>
<HIKETEIA IS NEVER ABOUT THE SUPPLICANT, PRINCESS-ONCE-GODDESS...>
<...BUT ALWAYS ABOUT THE SUPPLICATED.>

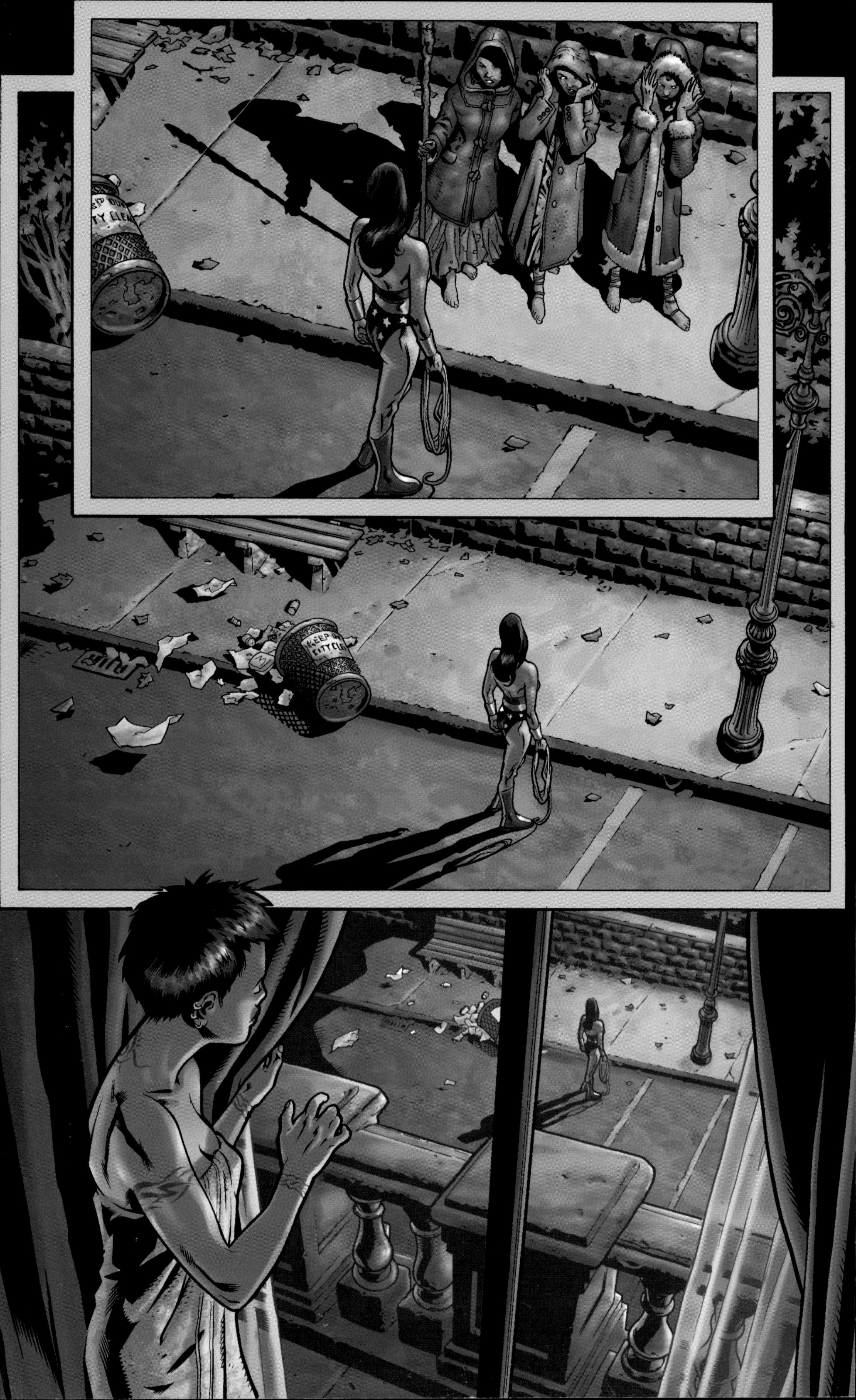

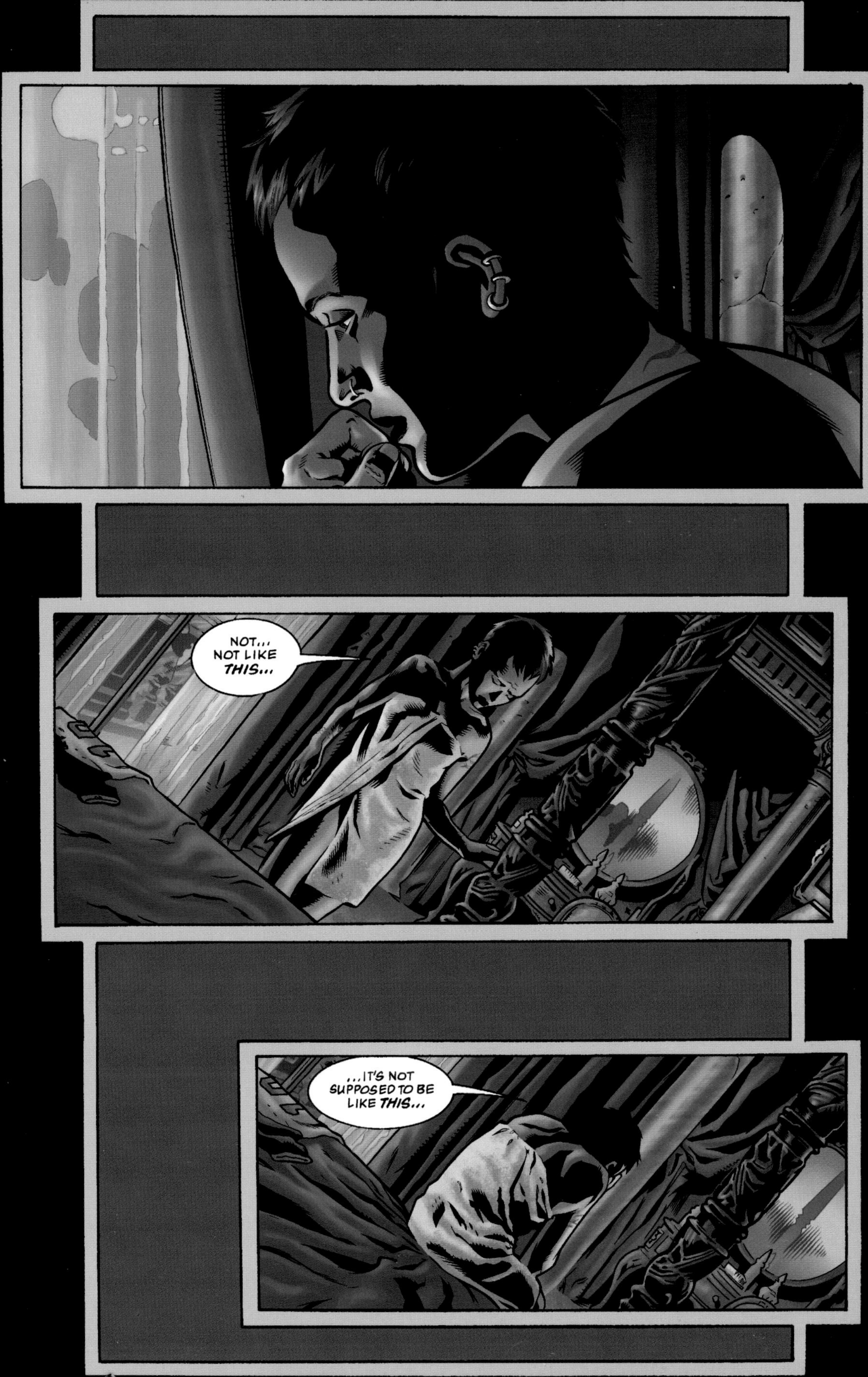
NOT... NOT LIKE THIS...
...IT'S NOT SUPPOSED TO BE LIKE THIS...

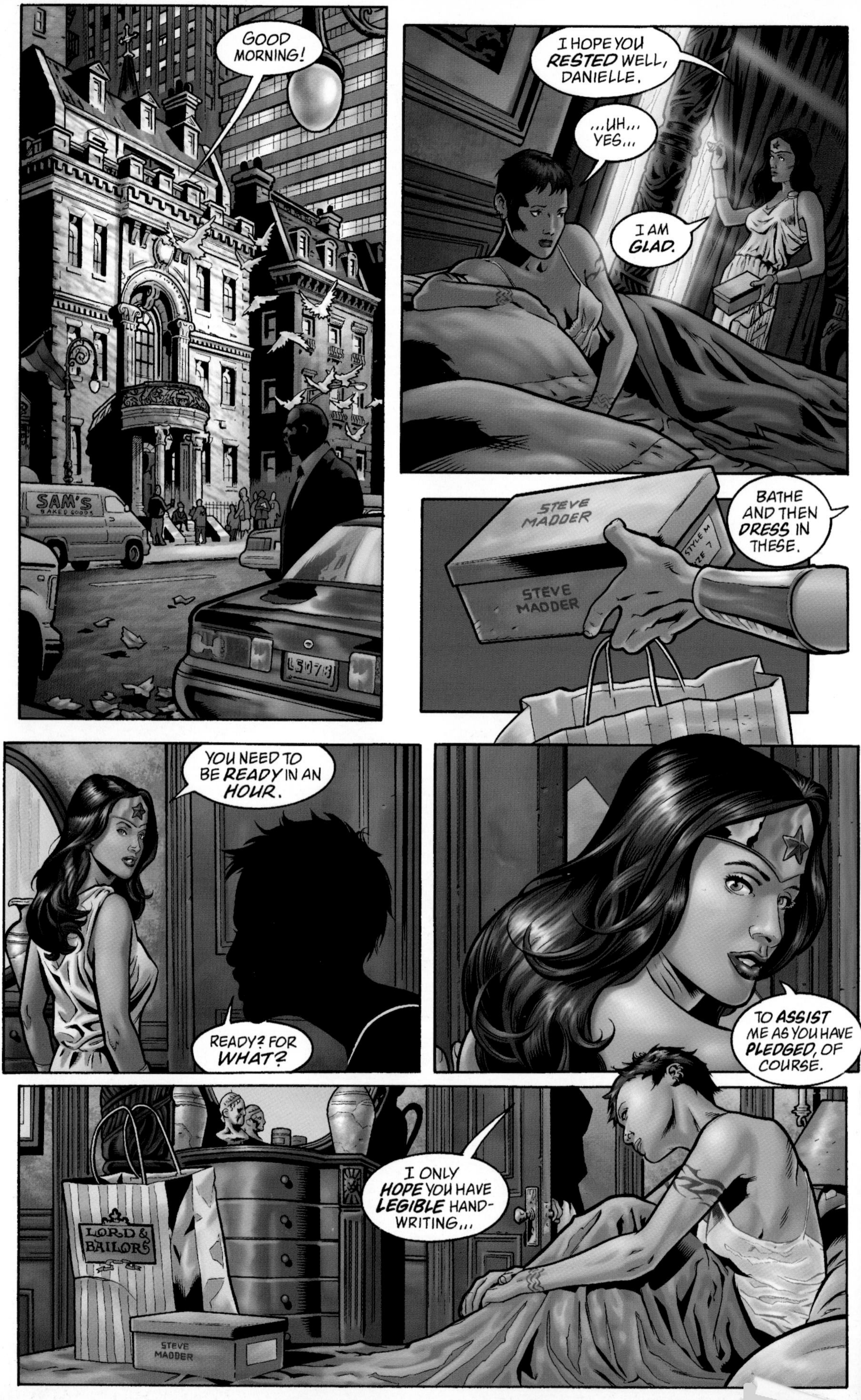
GOOD MORNING!
SAM'S BAKED GOODS
I HOPE YOU RESTED WELL, DANIELLE.
...UH... YES...
I AM GLAD.
STEVE MADDER
STEVE MADDER
BATHE AND THEN DRESS IN THESE.
YOU NEED TO BE READY IN AN HOUR.
READY? FOR WHAT?
TO ASSIST ME AS YOU HAVE PLEDGED, OF COURSE.
LORD & BAILOR
STEVE MADDER
I ONLY HOPE YOU HAVE LEGIBLE HAND-WRITING...

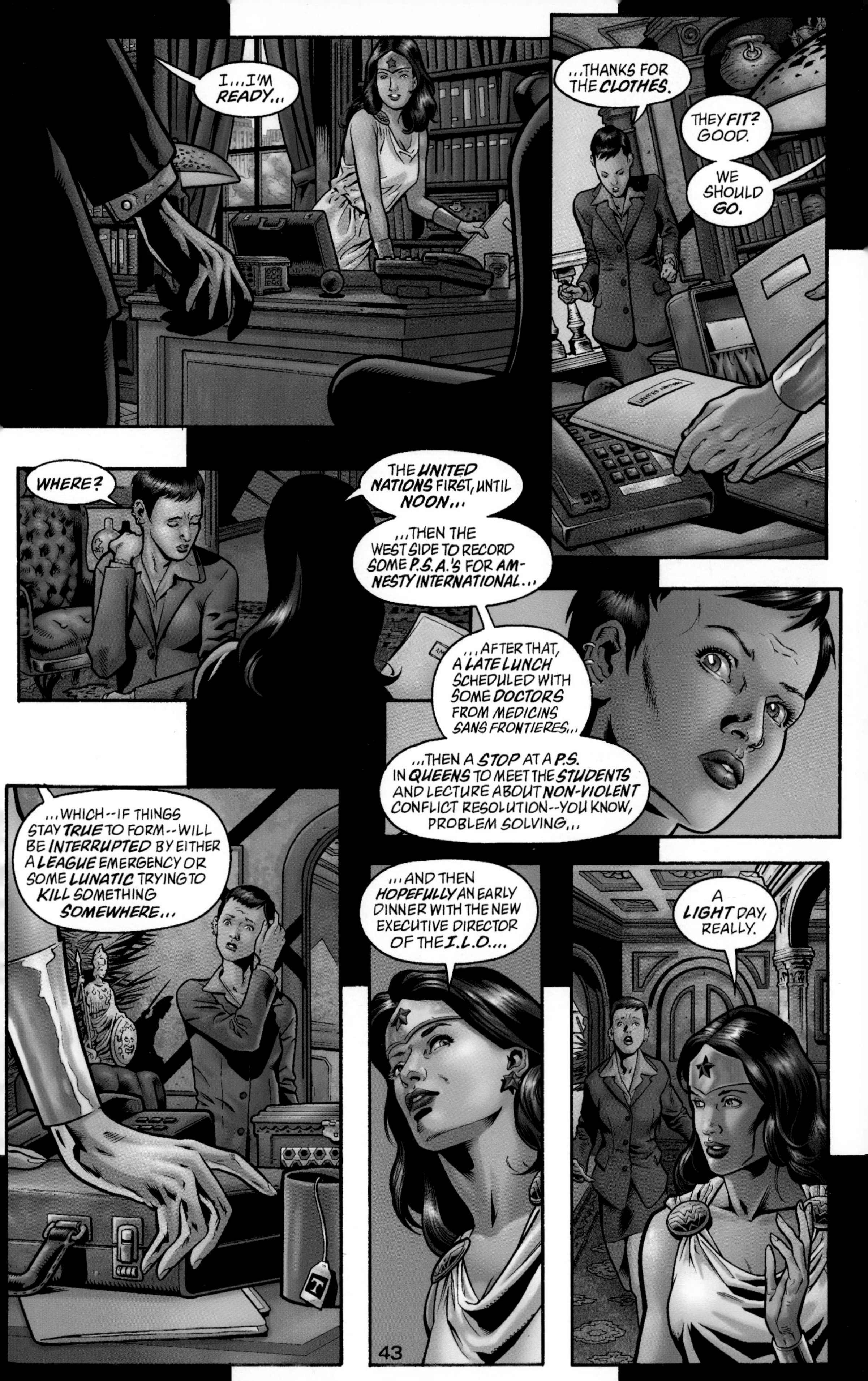
I...I'M READY...
...THANKS FOR THE CLOTHES.
THEY FIT? GOOD.
WE SHOULD GO.
WHERE?
THE UNITED NATIONS FIRST, UNTIL NOON...
...THEN THE WEST SIDE TO RECORD SOME P.S.A.'S FOR AMNESTY INTERNATIONAL...
...AFTER THAT, A LATE LUNCH SCHEDULED WITH SOME DOCTORS FROM MEDICINS SANS FRONTIERES...
...THEN A STOP AT A P.S. IN QUEENS TO MEET THE STUDENTS AND LECTURE ABOUT NON-VIOLENT CONFLICT RESOLUTION--YOU KNOW, PROBLEM SOLVING...
...WHICH--IF THINGS STAY TRUE TO FORM--WILL BE INTERRUPTED BY EITHER A LEAGUE EMERGENCY OR SOME LUNATIC TRYING TO KILL SOMETHING SOMEWHERE...
...AND THEN HOPEFULLY AN EARLY DINNER WITH THE NEW EXECUTIVE DIRECTOR OF THE I.L.O....
A LIGHT DAY, REALLY.

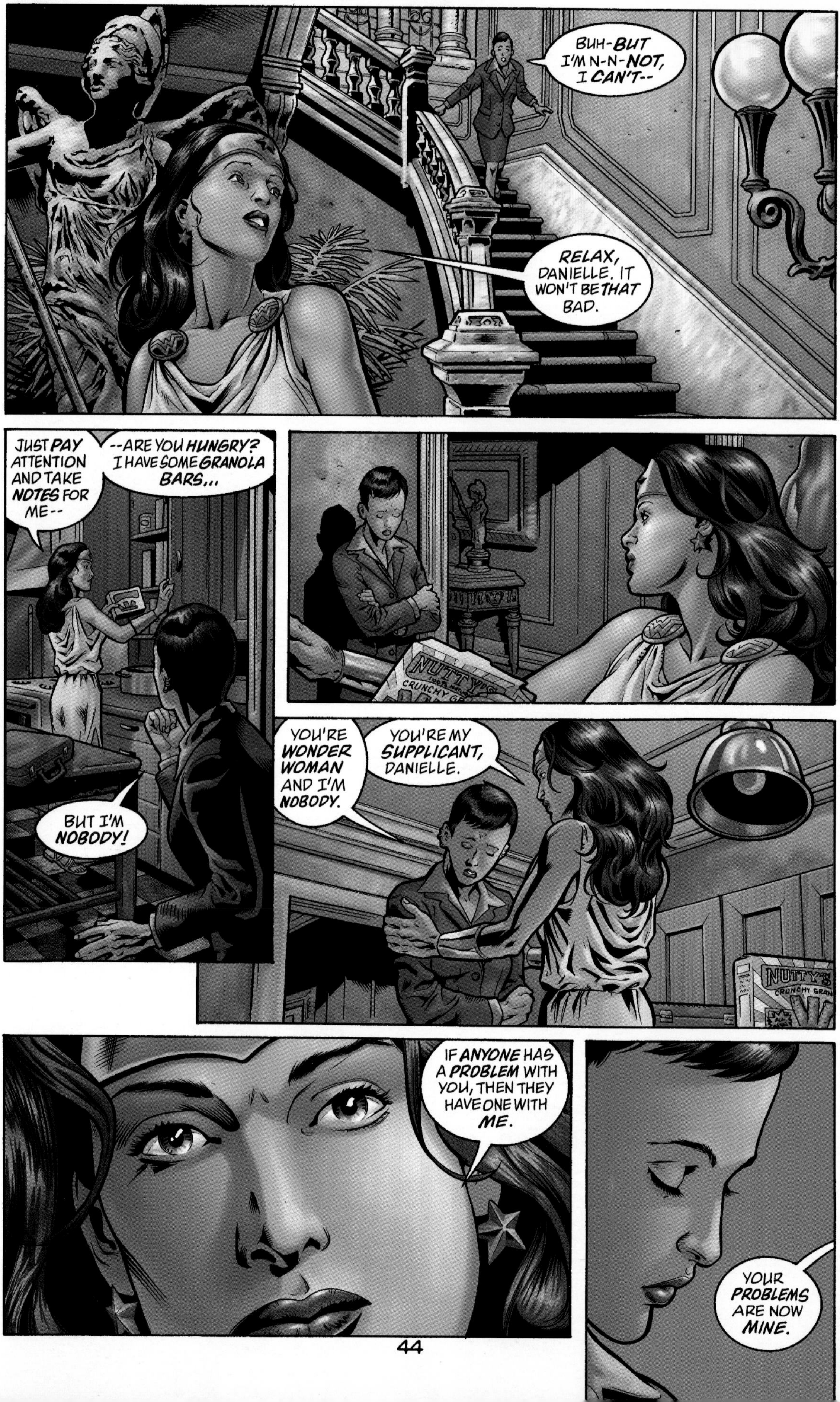
BUH-BUT I'M N-N-NOT, I CAN'T--
RELAX, DANIELLE. IT WON'T BE THAT BAD.
JUST PAY ATTENTION AND TAKE NOTES FOR ME--
--ARE YOU HUNGRY? I HAVE SOME GRANOLA BARS...
BUT I'M NOBODY!
NUTTY'S
CRUNCHY GR
YOU'RE WONDER WOMAN AND I'M NOBODY.
YOU'RE MY SUPPLICANT, DANIELLE.
NUTTY'S
CRUNCHY GRAN
IF ANYONE HAS A PROBLEM WITH YOU, THEN THEY HAVE ONE WITH ME.
YOUR PROBLEMS ARE NOW MINE.

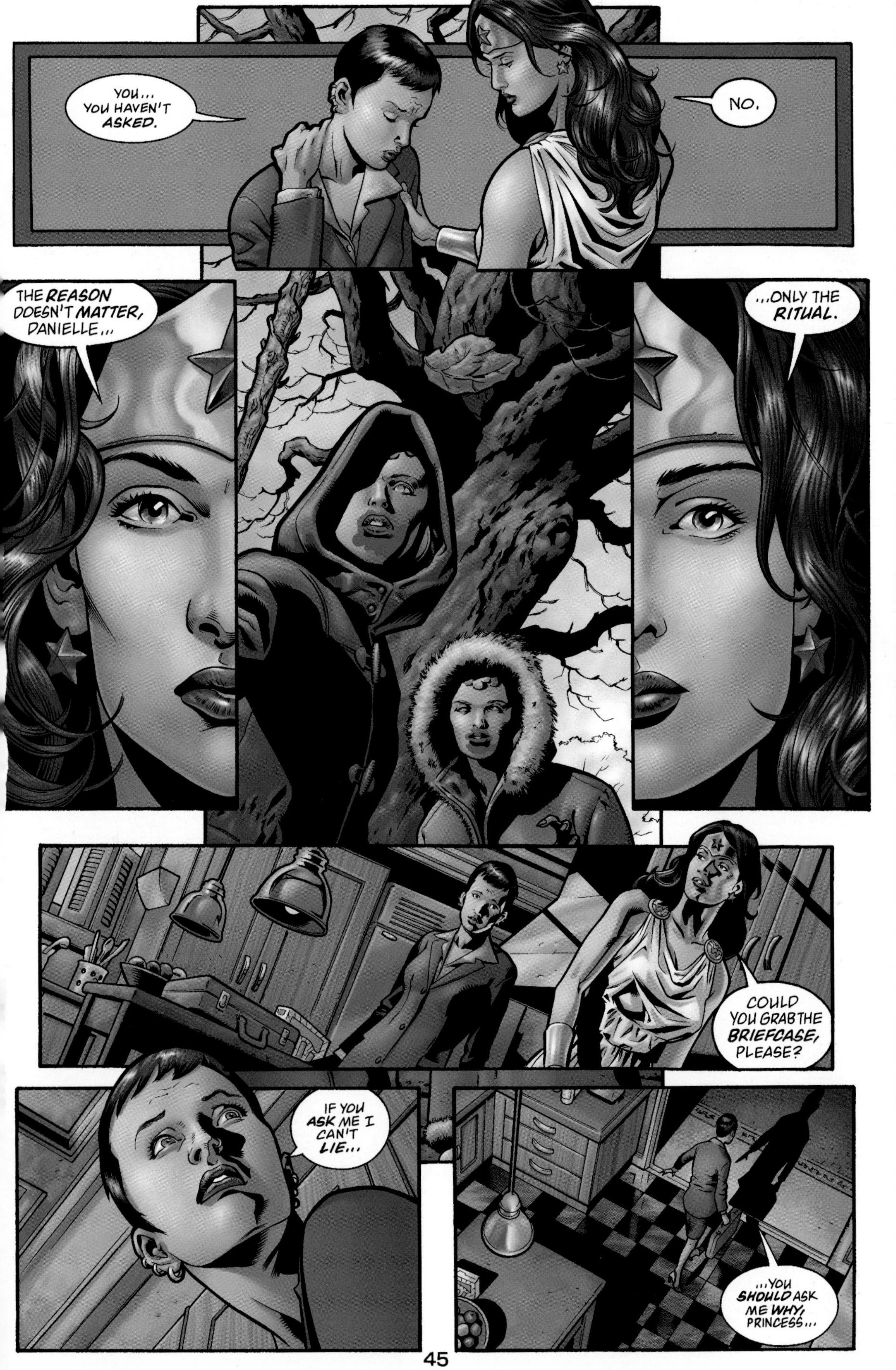
YOU... YOU HAVEN'T ASKED.
NO.
THE REASON DOESN'T MATTER, DANIELLE...
...ONLY THE RITUAL.
COULD YOU GRAB THE BRIEFCASE, PLEASE?
IF YOU ASK ME I CAN'T LIE...
...YOU SHOULD ASK ME WHY, PRINCESS...

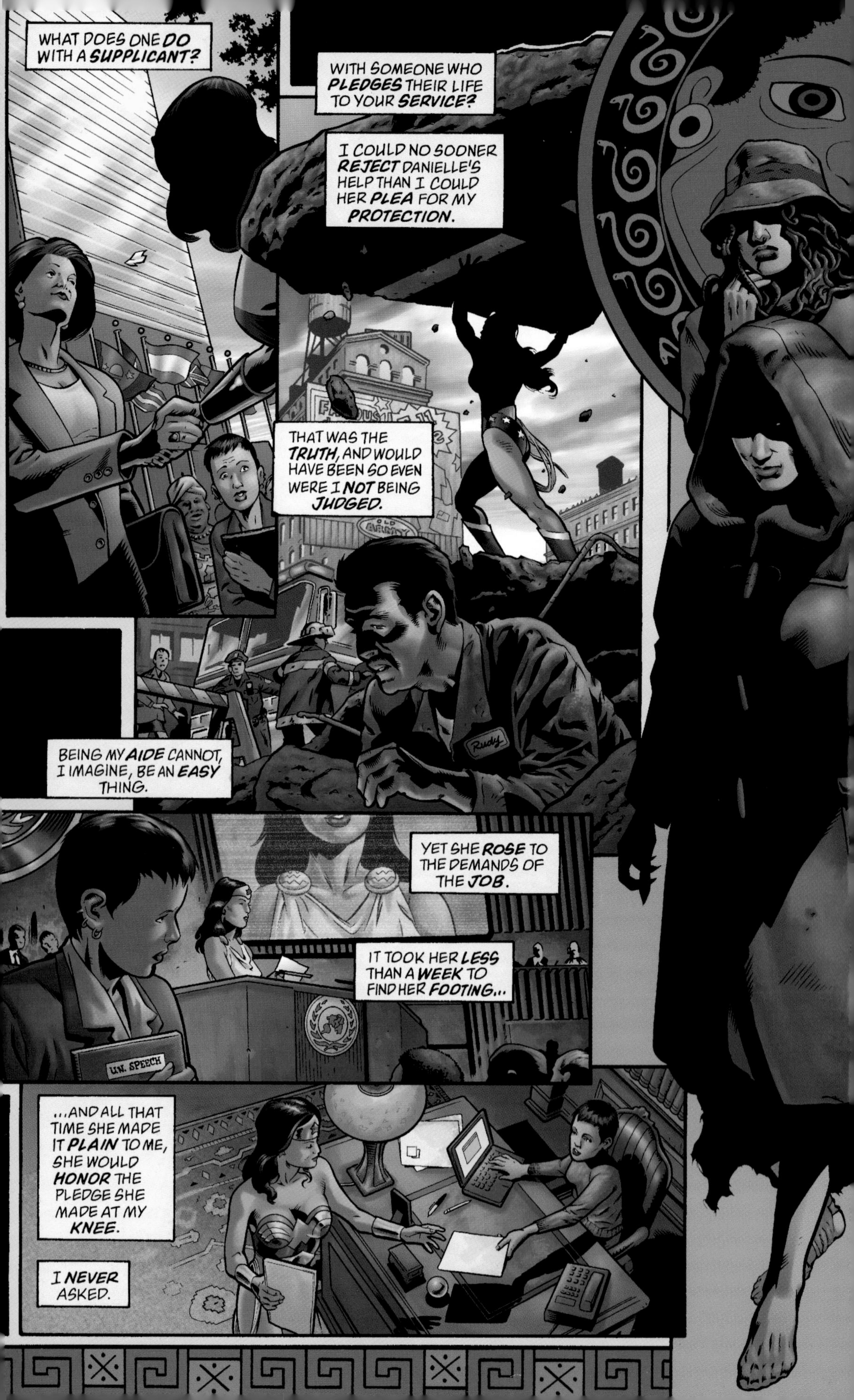
WHAT DOES ONE DO WITH A SUPPLICANT?
WITH SOMEONE WHO PLEDGES THEIR LIFE TO YOUR SERVICE?
I COULD NO SOONER REJECT DANIELLE'S HELP THAN I COULD HER PLEA FOR MY PROTECTION.
THAT WAS THE TRUTH, AND WOULD HAVE BEEN SO EVEN WERE I NOT BEING JUDGED.
Rudy
BEING MY AIDE CANNOT, I IMAGINE, BE AN EASY THING.
YET SHE ROSE TO THE DEMANDS OF THE JOB.
IT TOOK HER LESS THAN A WEEK TO FIND HER FOOTING...
U.N. SPEECH
...AND ALL THAT TIME SHE MADE IT PLAIN TO ME, SHE WOULD HONOR THE PLEDGE SHE MADE AT MY KNEE.
I NEVER ASKED.

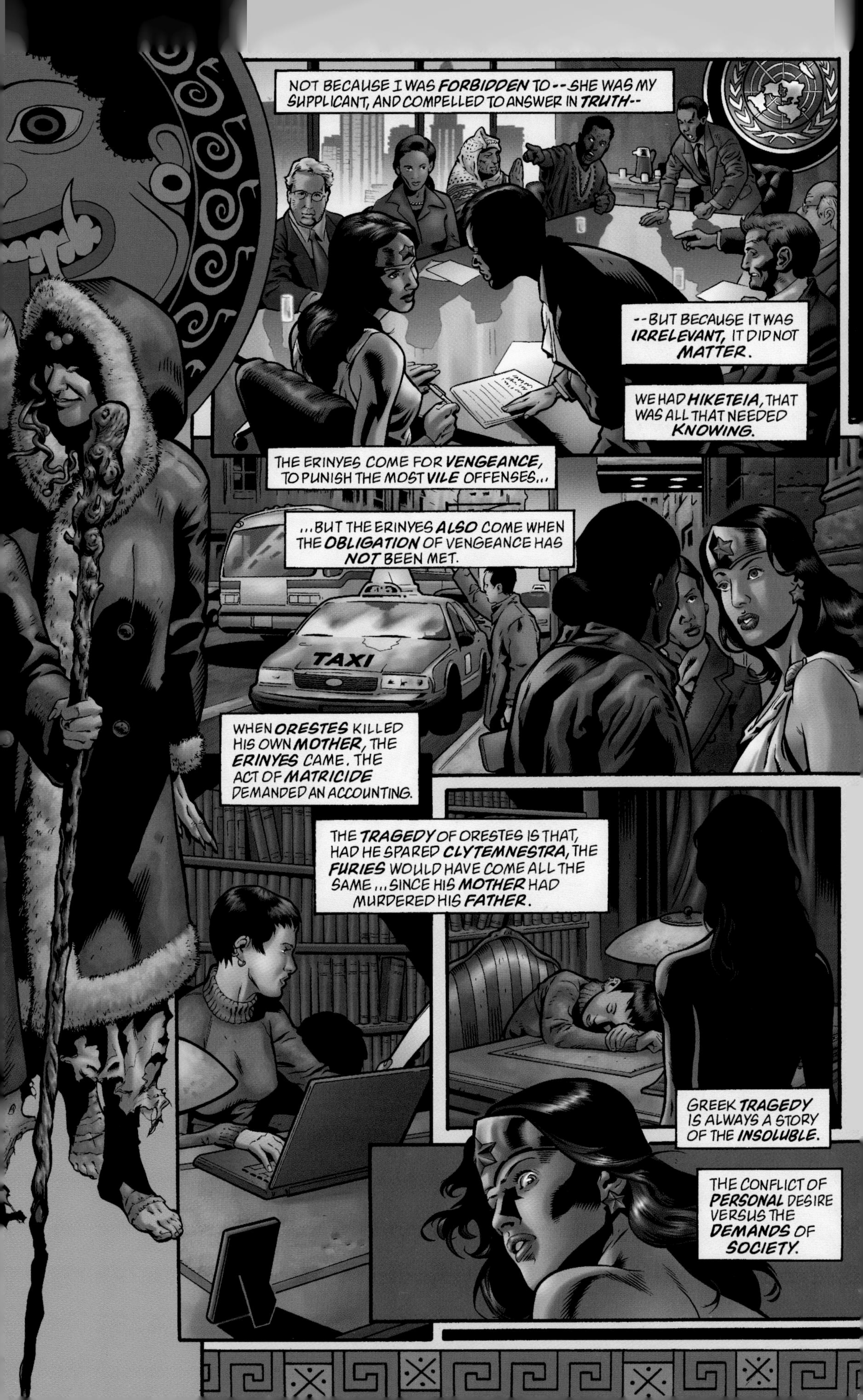
NOT BECAUSE I WAS FORBIDDEN TO -- SHE WAS MY SUPPLICANT, AND COMPELLED TO ANSWER IN TRUTH--
--BUT BECAUSE IT WAS IRRELEVANT, IT DID NOT MATTER.
WE HAD HIKETEIA, THAT WAS ALL THAT NEEDED KNOWING.
THE ERINYES COME FOR VENGEANCE, TO PUNISH THE MOST VILE OFFENSES...
...BUT THE ERINYES ALSO COME WHEN THE OBLIGATION OF VENGEANCE HAS NOT BEEN MET.
TAXI
WHEN ORESTES KILLED HIS OWN MOTHER, THE ERINYES CAME. THE ACT OF MATRICIDE DEMANDED AN ACCOUNTING.
THE TRAGEDY OF ORESTES IS THAT, HAD HE SPARED CLYTEMNESTRA, THE FURIES WOULD HAVE COME ALL THE SAME ... SINCE HIS MOTHER HAD MURDERED HIS FATHER.
GREEK TRAGEDY IS ALWAYS A STORY OF THE INSOLUBLE.
THE CONFLICT OF PERSONAL DESIRE VERSUS THE DEMANDS OF SOCIETY.

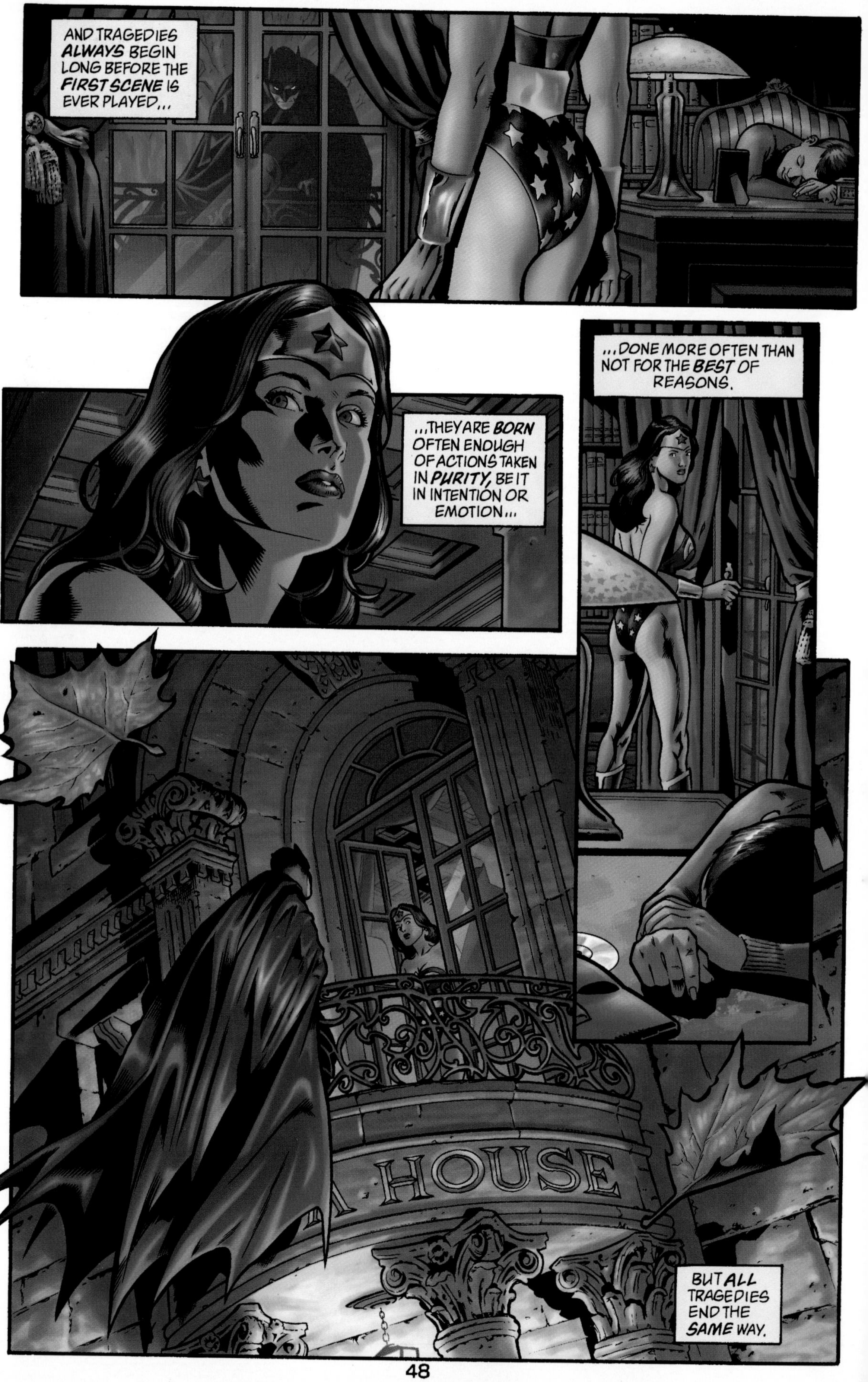
AND TRAGEDIES ALWAYS BEGIN LONG BEFORE THE FIRST SCENE IS EVER PLAYED...
...THEY ARE BORN OFTEN ENOUGH OF ACTIONS TAKEN IN PURITY, BE IT IN INTENTION OR EMOTION...
...DONE MORE OFTEN THAN NOT FOR THE BEST OF REASONS.
A HOUSE
BUT ALL TRAGEDIES END THE SAME WAY.

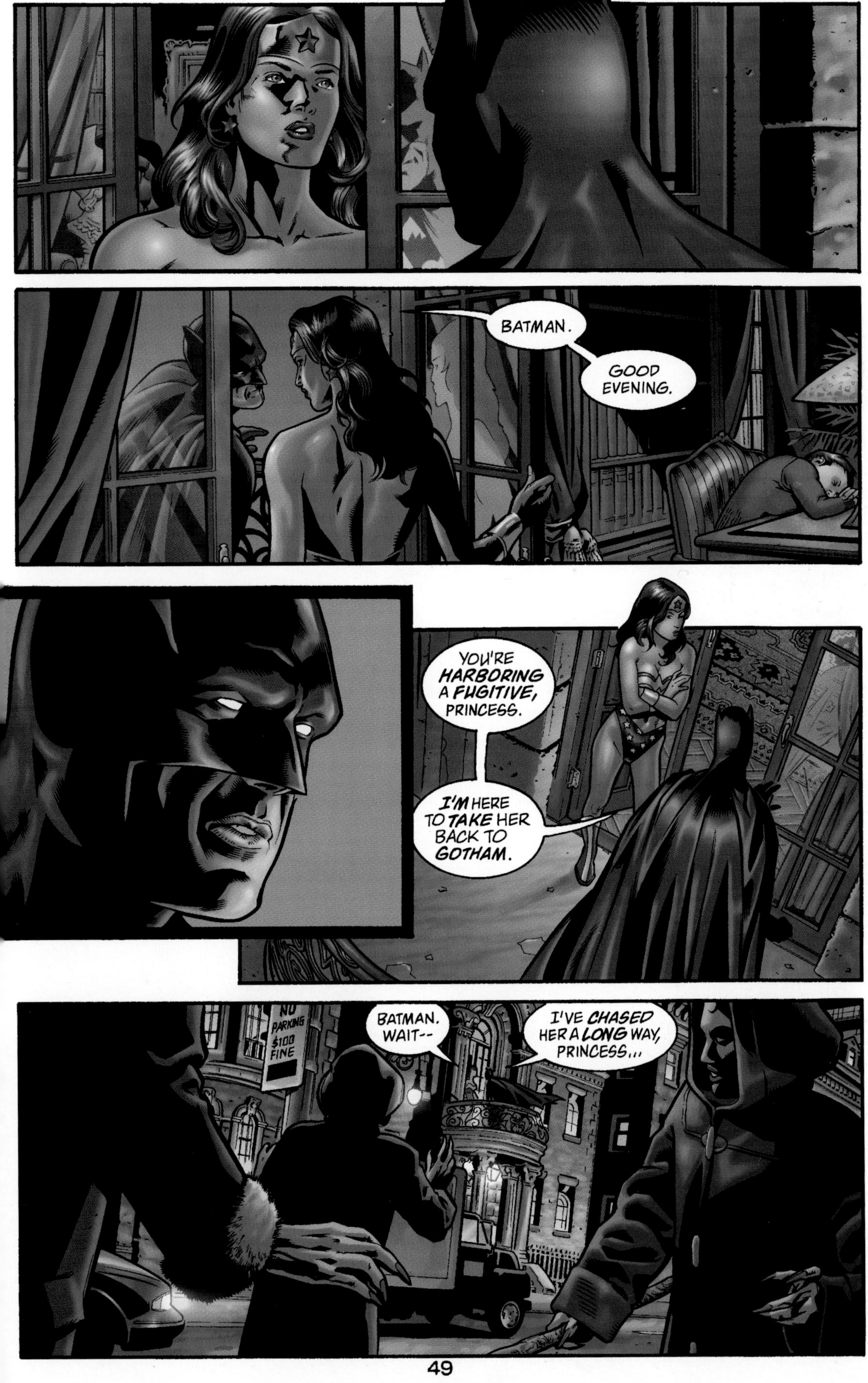
BATMAN.
GOOD EVENING.
YOU'RE HARBORING A FUGITIVE, PRINCESS.
I'M HERE TO TAKE HER BACK TO GOTHAM.
NO PARKING $100 FINE
BATMAN. WAIT--
I'VE CHASED HER A LONG WAY, PRINCESS...

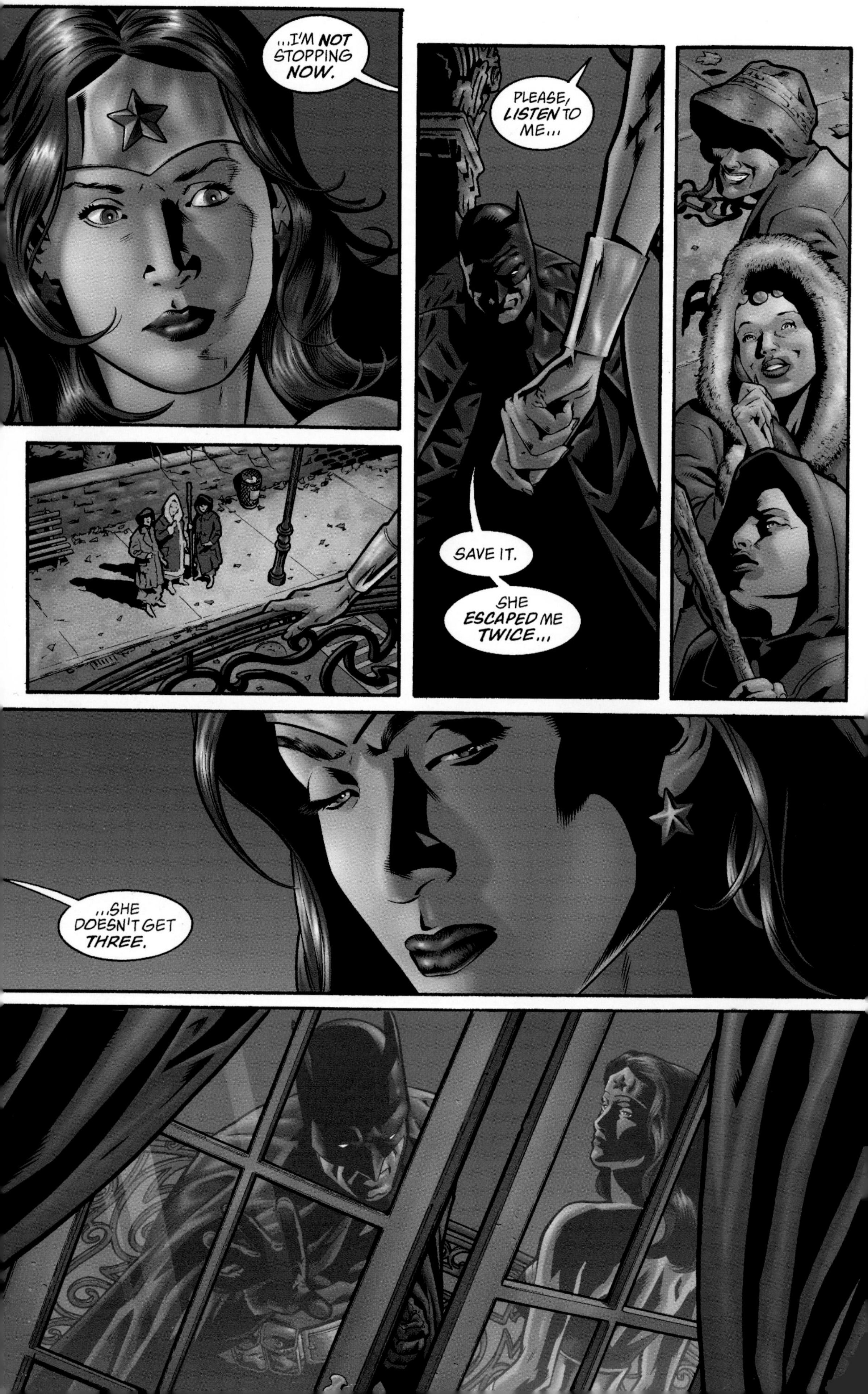
...I'M NOT STOPPING NOW.
PLEASE, LISTEN TO ME...
SAVE IT.
SHE ESCAPED ME TWICE...
...SHE DOESN'T GET THREE.

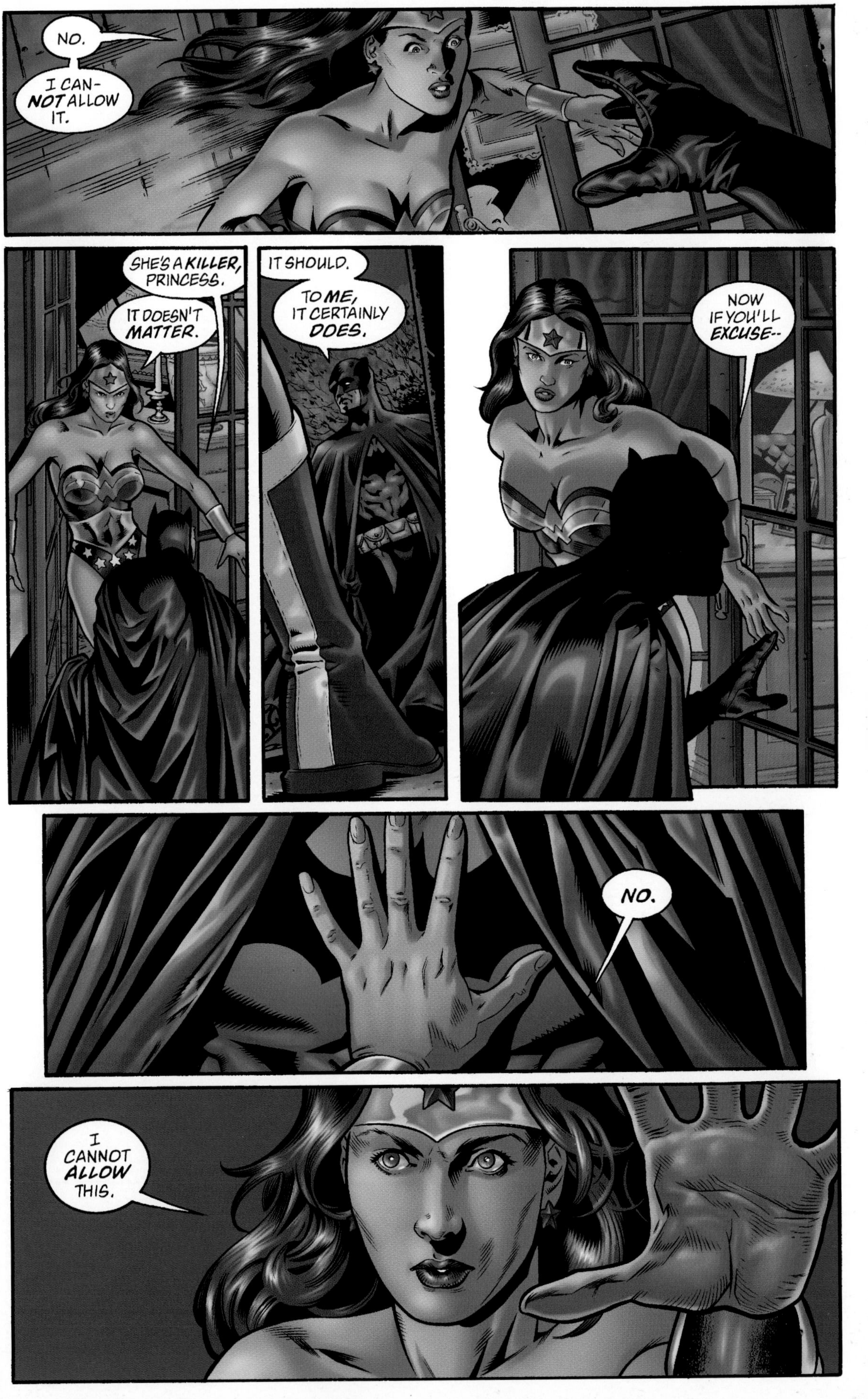
NO.
I CAN-NOT ALLOW IT.
SHE'S A KILLER, PRINCESS.
IT DOESN'T MATTER.
IT SHOULD.
TO ME, IT CERTAINLY DOES.
NOW IF YOU'LL EXCUSE--
NO.
I CANNOT ALLOW THIS.

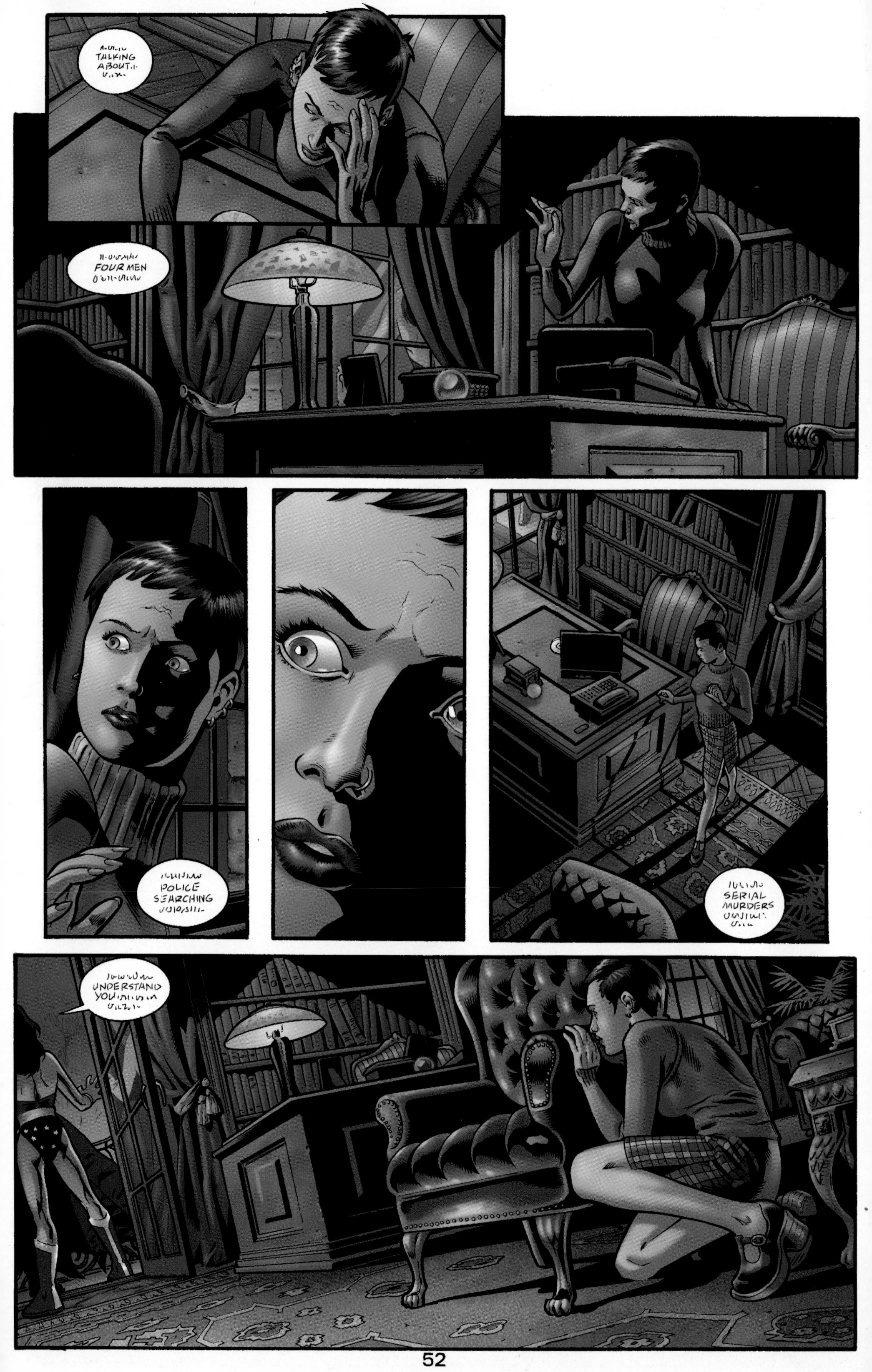
TALKING ABOUT
FOUR MEN
POLICE SEARCHING
SERIAL MURDERS
UNDERSTAND YOU

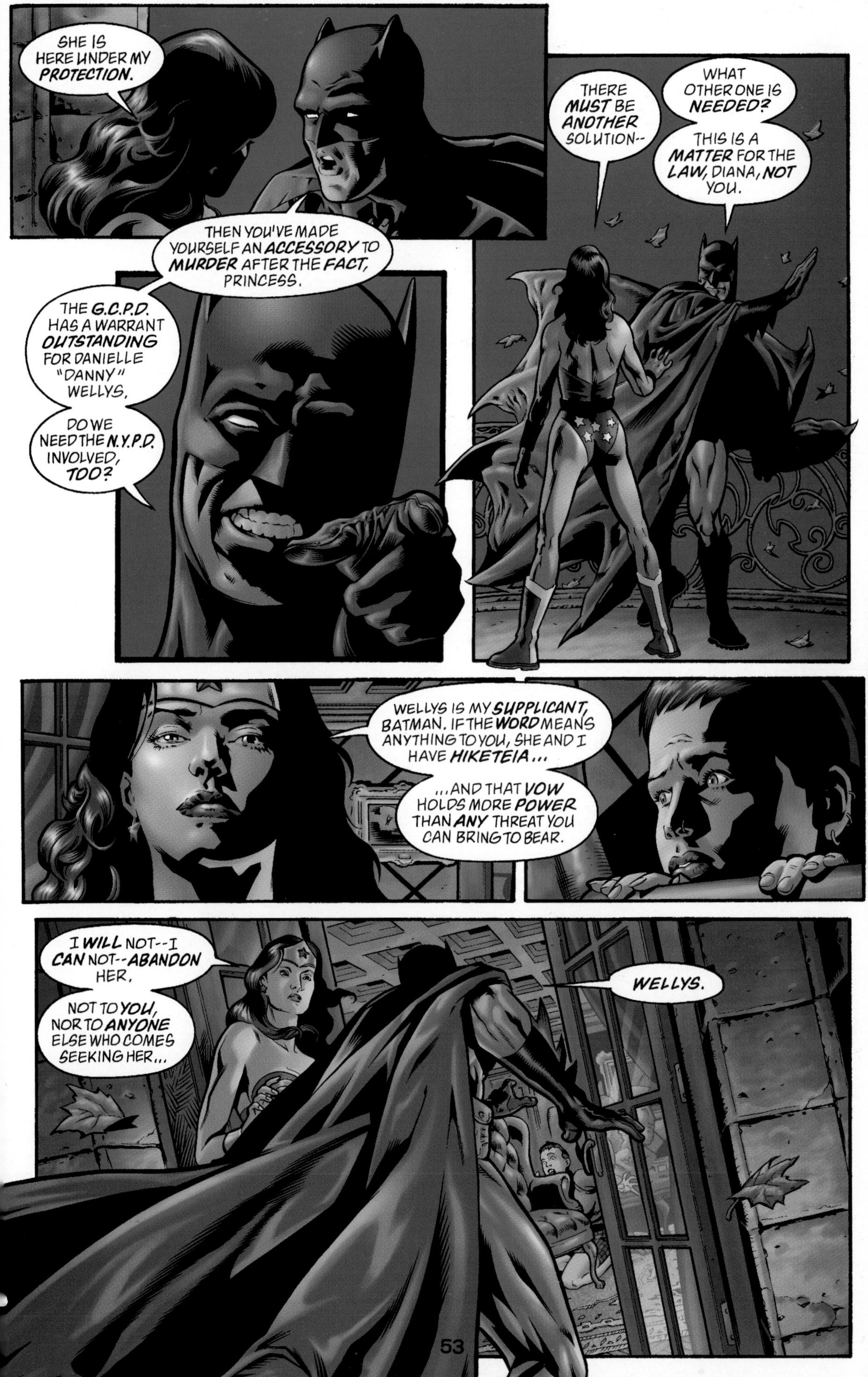
SHE IS HERE UNDER MY PROTECTION.
THERE MUST BE ANOTHER SOLUTION--
WHAT OTHER ONE IS NEEDED?
THIS IS A MATTER FOR THE LAW, DIANA, NOT YOU.
THEN YOU'VE MADE YOURSELF AN ACCESSORY TO MURDER AFTER THE FACT, PRINCESS.
THE G.C.P.D. HAS A WARRANT OUTSTANDING FOR DANIELLE "DANNY" WELLYS.
DO WE NEED THE N.Y.P.D. INVOLVED, TOO?
WELLYS IS MY SUPPLICANT, BATMAN. IF THE WORD MEANS ANYTHING TO YOU, SHE AND I HAVE HIKETEIA...
...AND THAT VOW HOLDS MORE POWER THAN ANY THREAT YOU CAN BRING TO BEAR.
I WILL NOT--I CAN NOT--ABANDON HER.
NOT TO YOU, NOR TO ANYONE ELSE WHO COMES SEEKING HER...
WELLYS.

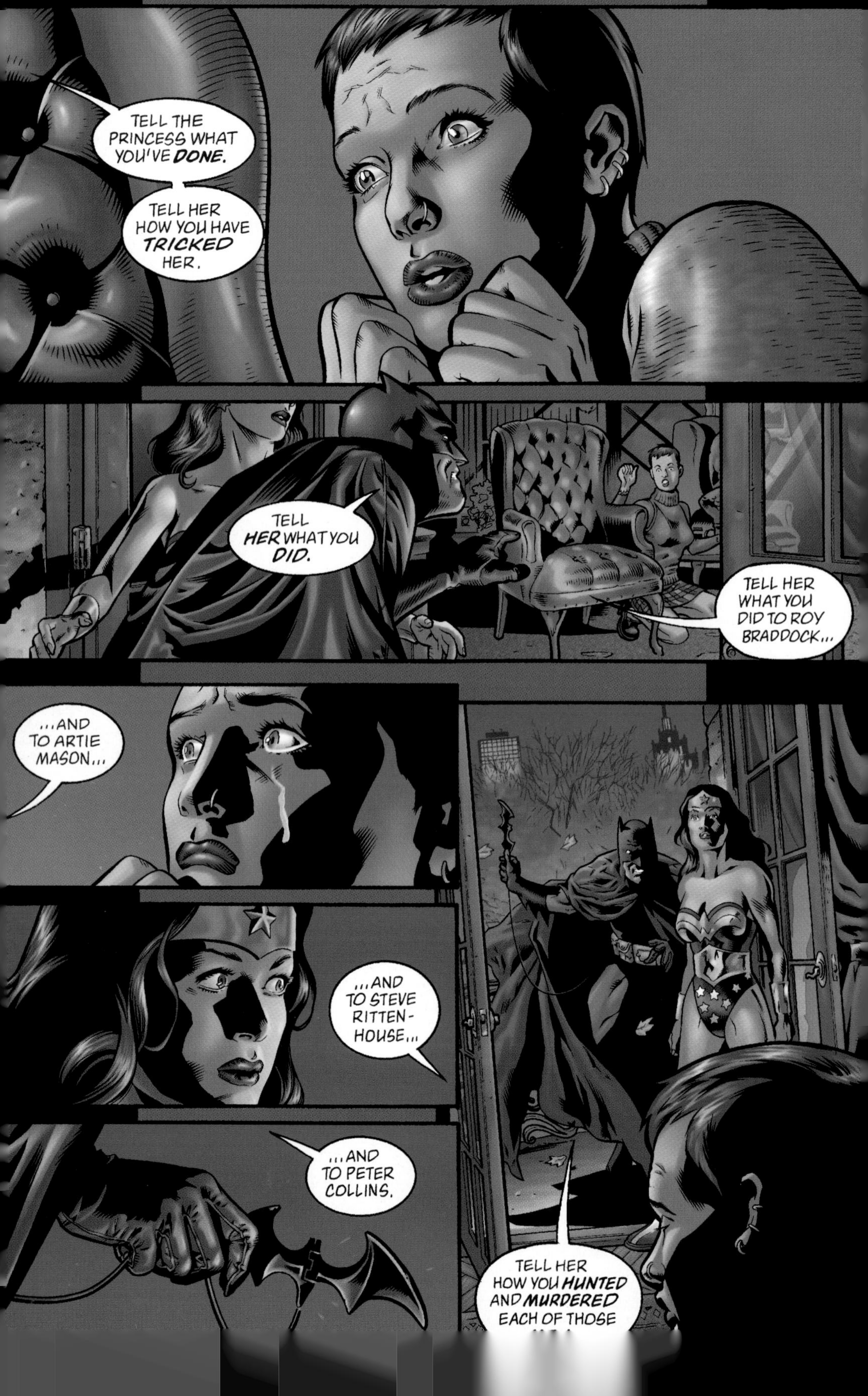
TELL THE PRINCESS WHAT YOU'VE **DONE.**
TELL HER HOW YOU HAVE **TRICKED** HER.
TELL **HER** WHAT YOU **DID.**
TELL HER WHAT YOU DID TO ROY BRADDOCK...
...AND TO ARTIE MASON...
...AND TO STEVE RITTEN-HOUSE...
...AND TO PETER COLLINS.
TELL HER HOW YOU **HUNTED** AND **MURDERED** EACH OF THOSE

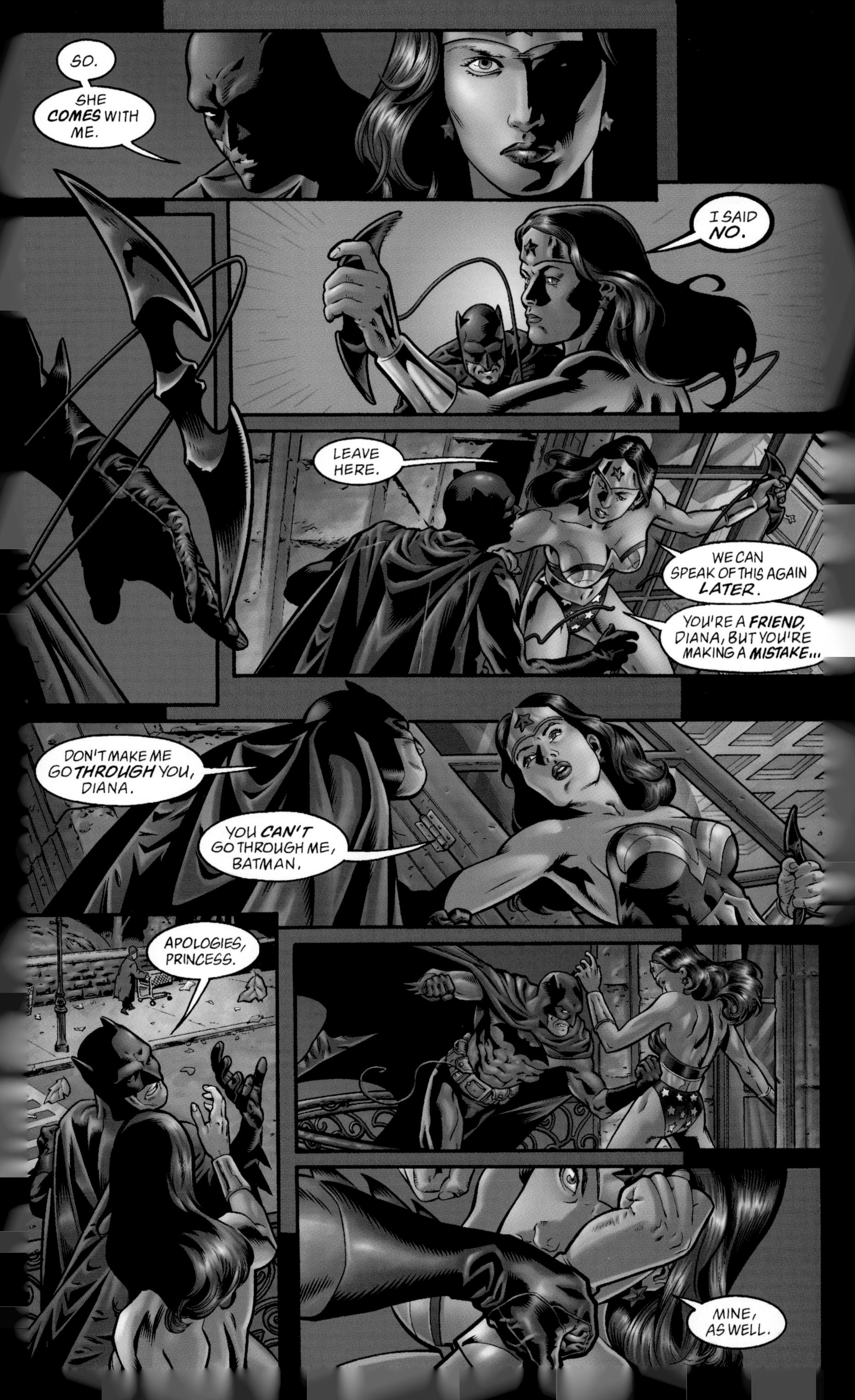
SO. SHE COMES WITH ME.
I SAID NO.
LEAVE HERE.
WE CAN SPEAK OF THIS AGAIN LATER.
YOU'RE A FRIEND, DIANA, BUT YOU'RE MAKING A MISTAKE...
DON'T MAKE ME GO THROUGH YOU, DIANA.
YOU CAN'T GO THROUGH ME, BATMAN.
APOLOGIES, PRINCESS.
MINE, AS WELL.

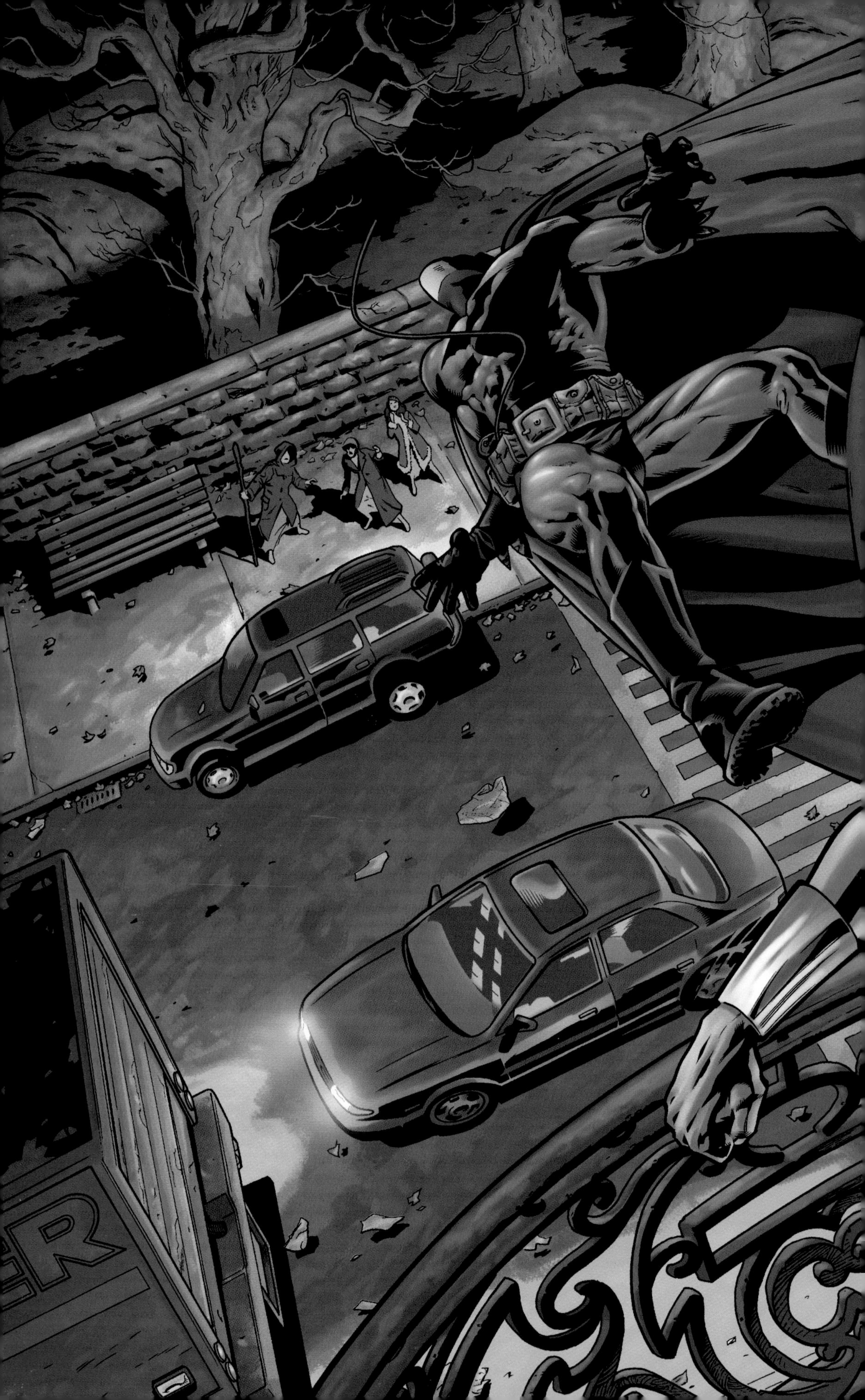

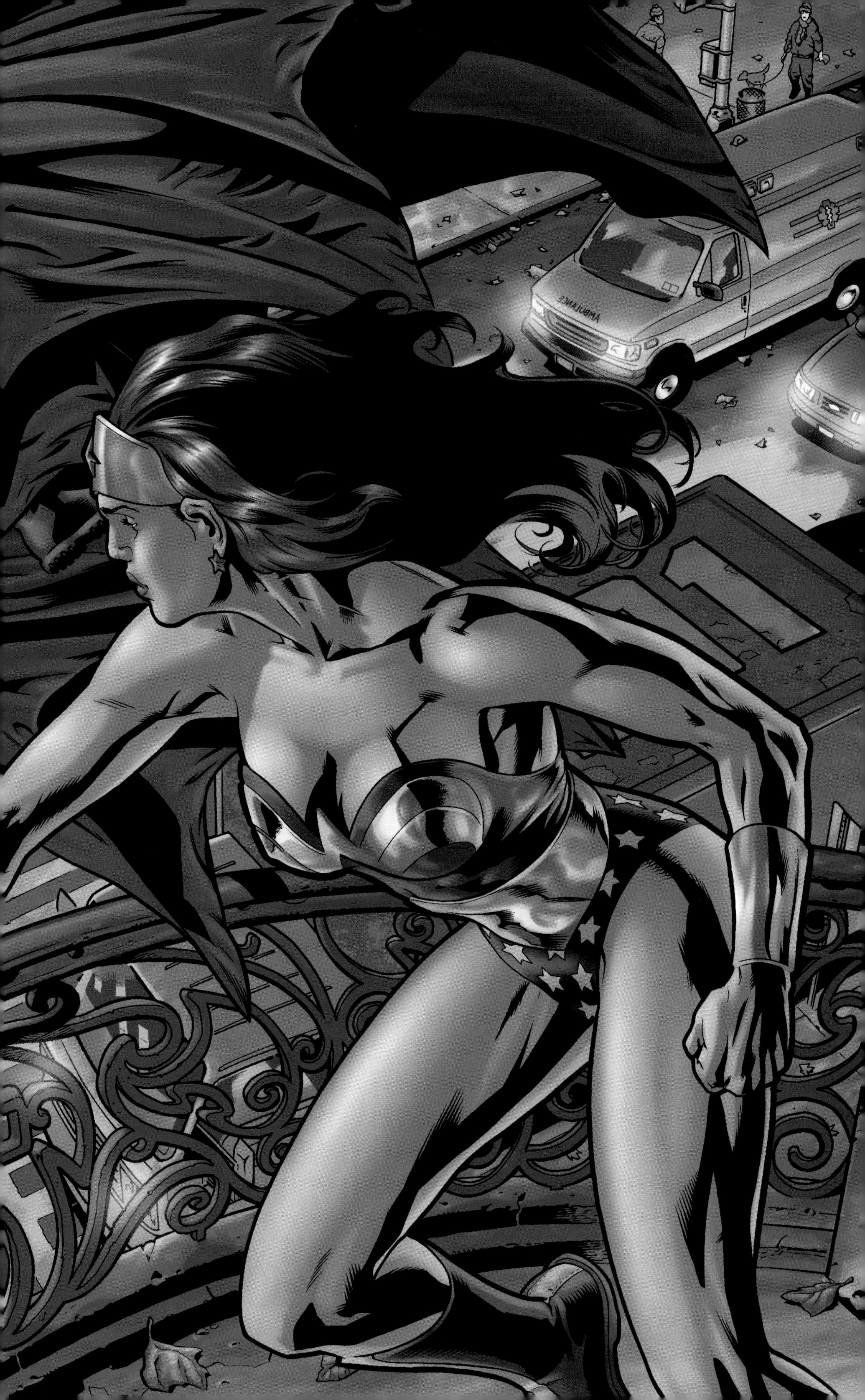
AMBULANCE

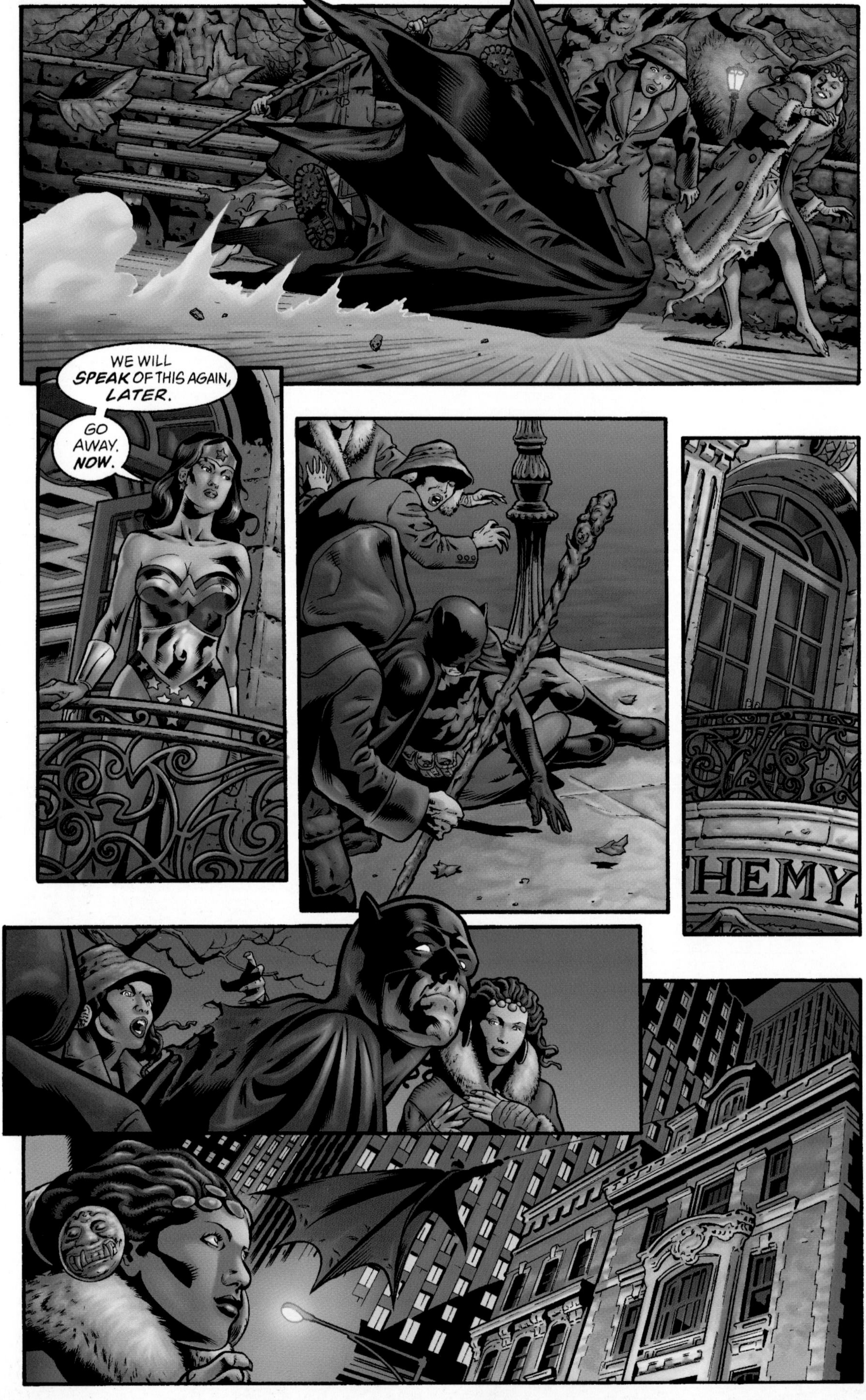
WE WILL SPEAK OF THIS AGAIN, LATER.
GO AWAY. NOW.
HEMY

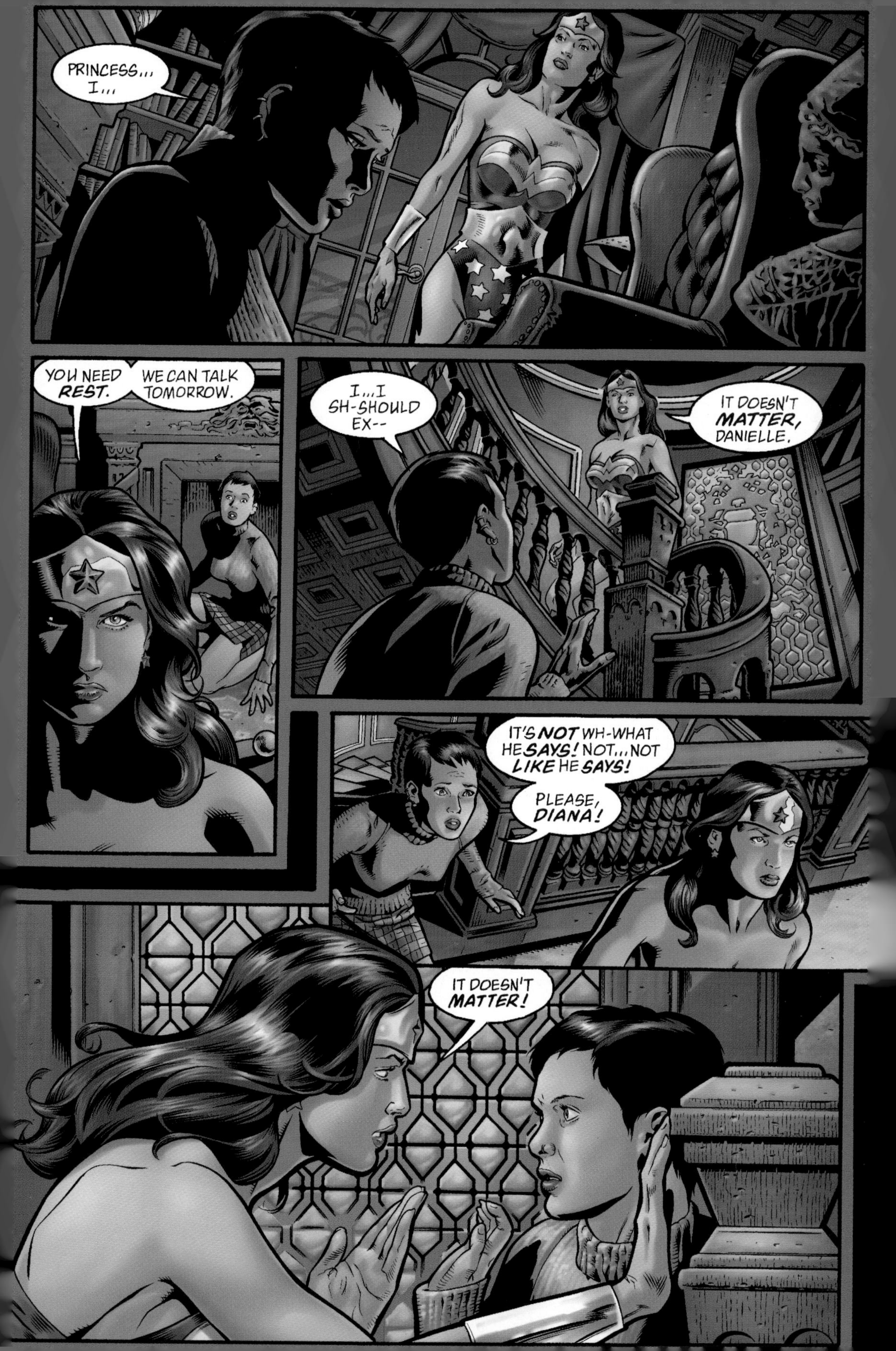
PRINCESS... I...
YOU NEED REST.
WE CAN TALK TOMORROW.
I...I SH-SHOULD EX--
IT DOESN'T MATTER, DANIELLE.
IT'S NOT WH-WHAT HE SAYS! NOT...NOT LIKE HE SAYS!
PLEASE, DIANA!
IT DOESN'T MATTER!

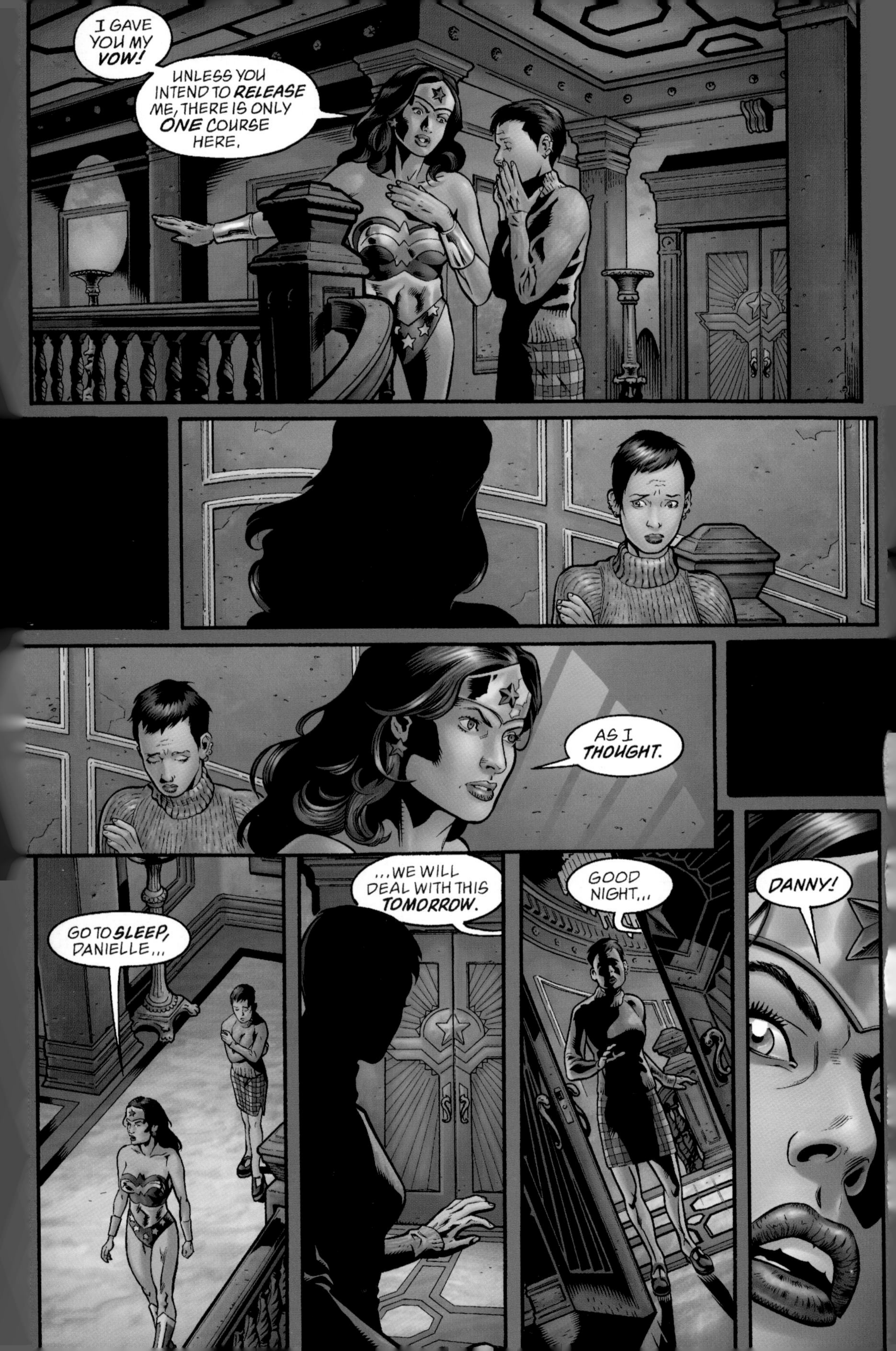
I GAVE YOU MY VOW!
UNLESS YOU INTEND TO RELEASE ME, THERE IS ONLY ONE COURSE HERE.
AS I THOUGHT.
GO TO SLEEP, DANIELLE...
...WE WILL DEAL WITH THIS TOMORROW.
GOOD NIGHT...
DANNY!

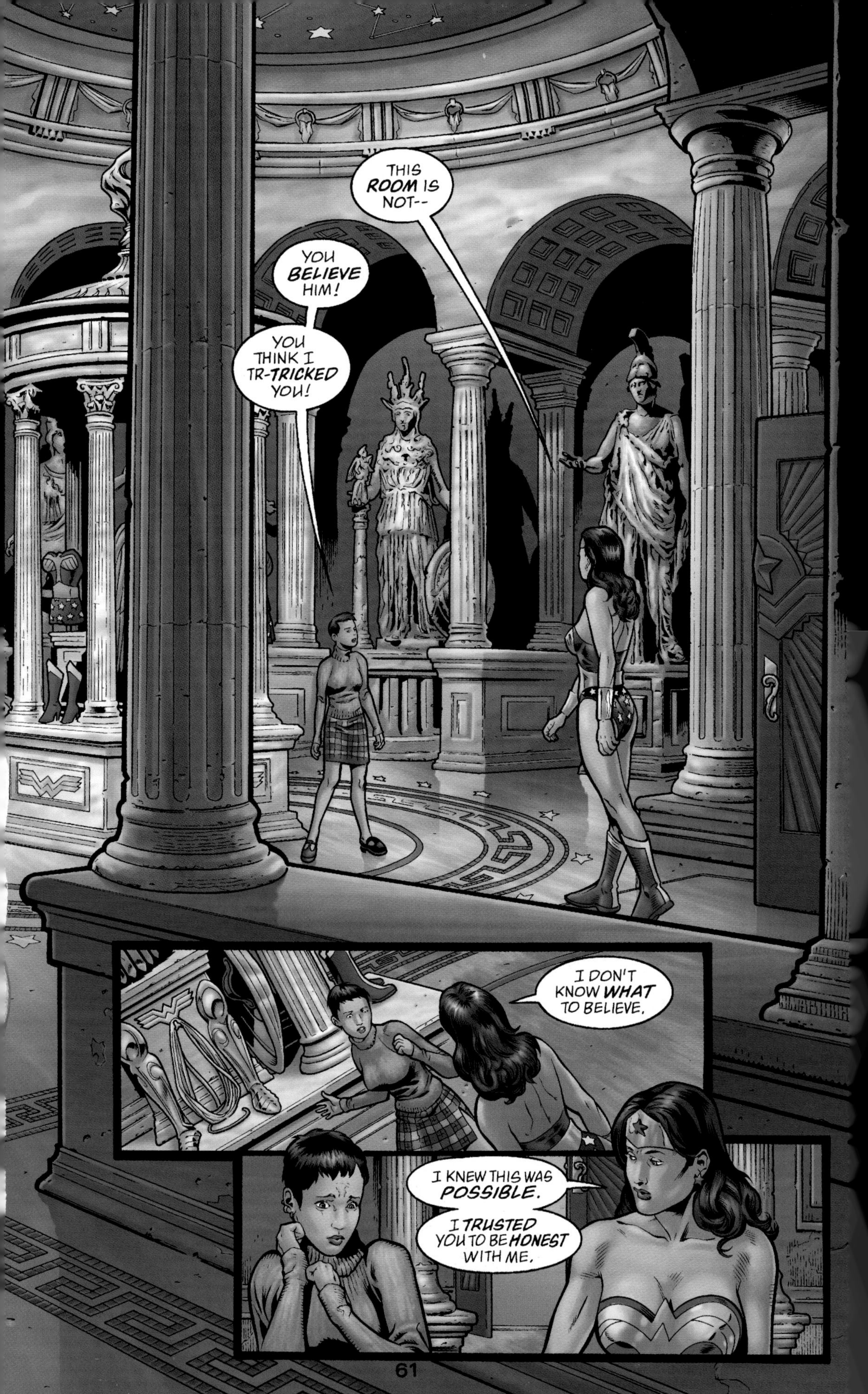
THIS ROOM IS NOT--
YOU BELIEVE HIM!
YOU THINK I TR-TRICKED YOU!
I DON'T KNOW WHAT TO BELIEVE.
I KNEW THIS WAS POSSIBLE.
I TRUSTED YOU TO BE HONEST WITH ME.

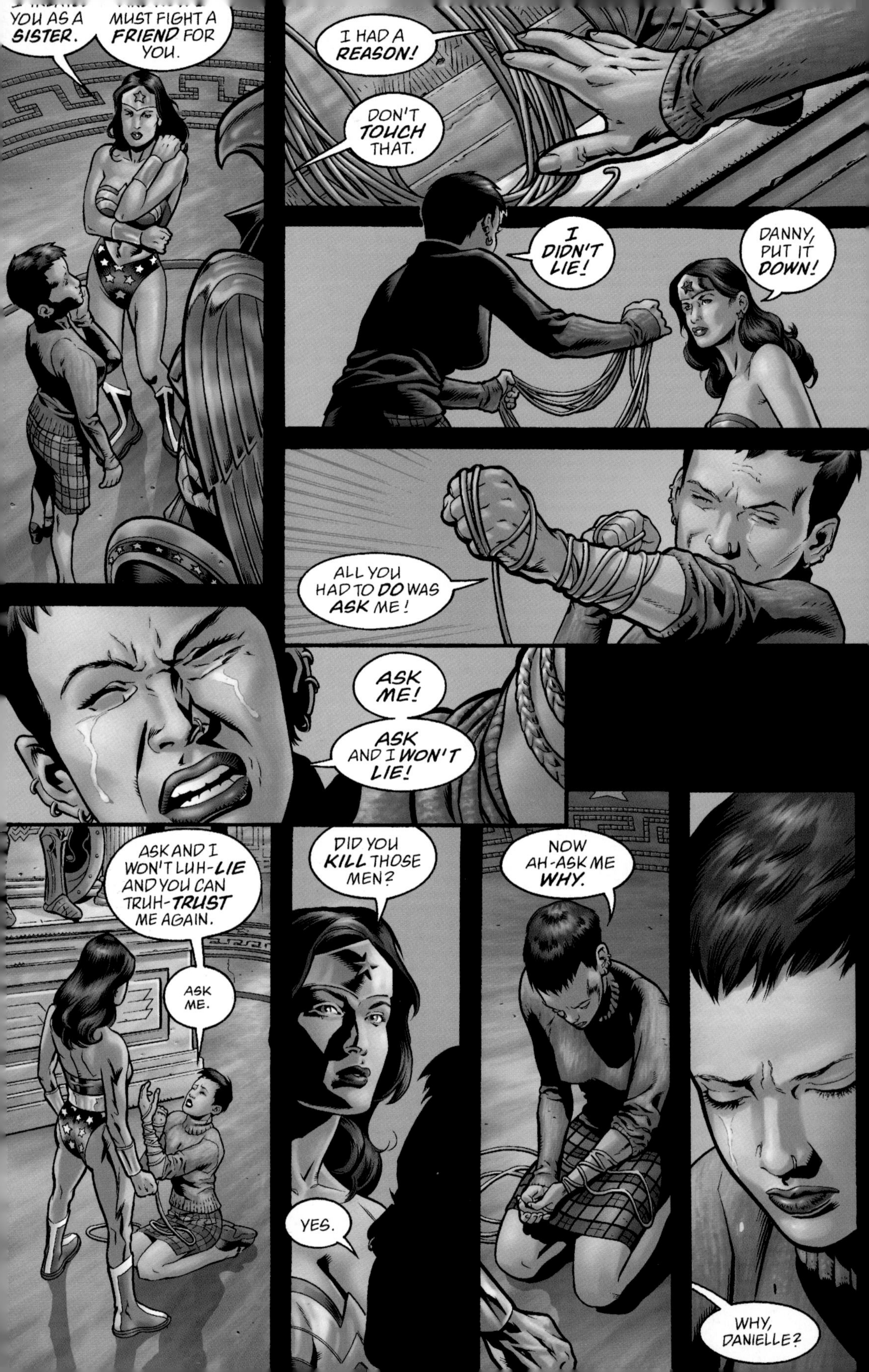
YOU AS A SISTER.
MUST FIGHT A FRIEND FOR YOU.
I HAD A REASON!
DON'T TOUCH THAT.
I DIDN'T LIE!
DANNY, PUT IT DOWN!
ALL YOU HAD TO DO WAS ASK ME!
ASK ME!
ASK AND I WON'T LIE!
ASK AND I WON'T LUH-LIE AND YOU CAN TRUH-TRUST ME AGAIN.
ASK ME.
DID YOU KILL THOSE MEN?
YES.
NOW AH-ASK ME WHY.
WHY, DANIELLE?

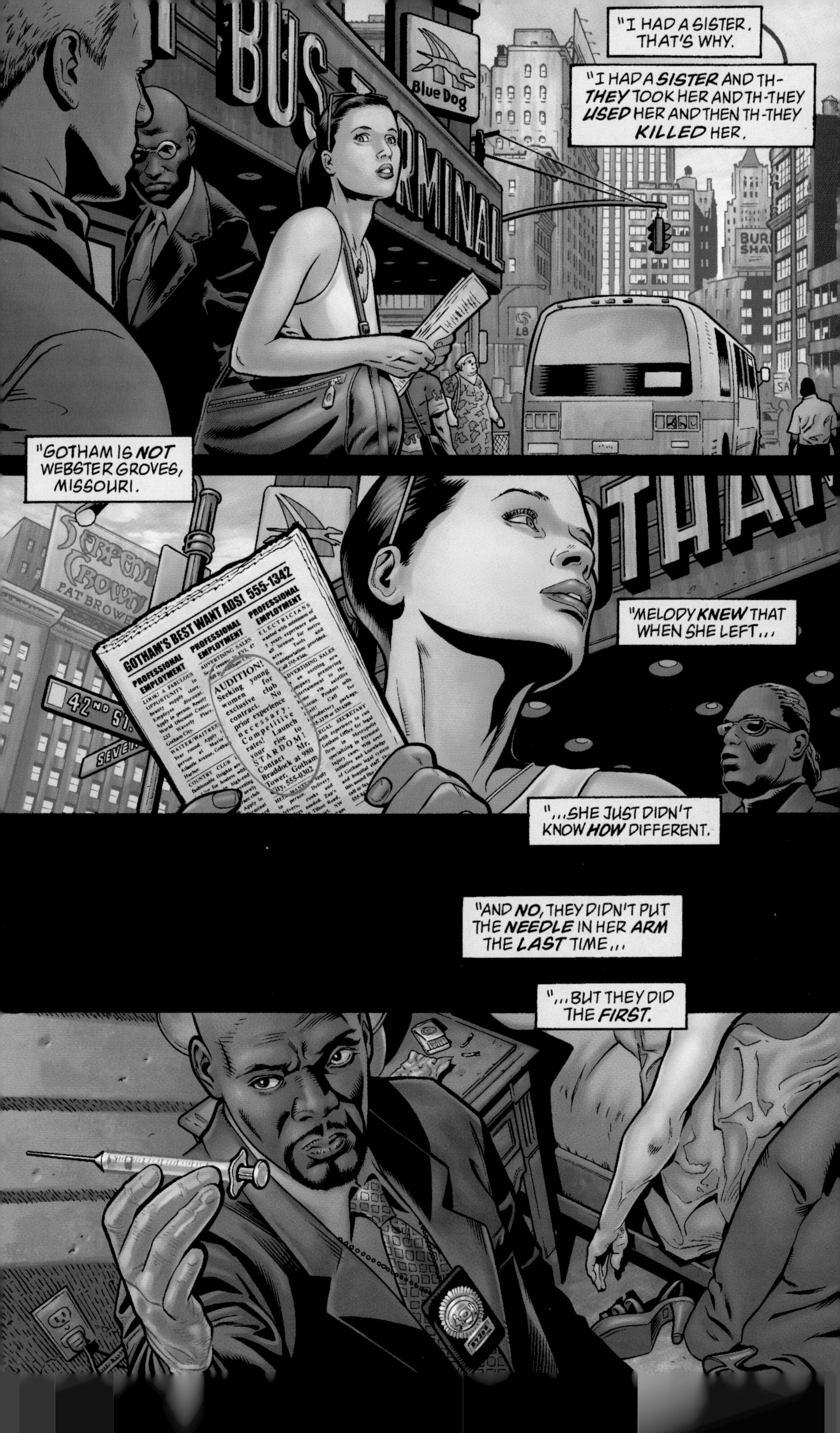
"I HAD A SISTER. THAT'S WHY.
"I HAD A SISTER AND TH- THEY TOOK HER AND TH-THEY USED HER AND THEN TH-THEY KILLED HER.
Blue Dog
"GOTHAM IS NOT WEBSTER GROVES, MISSOURI.
GOTHAM'S BEST WANT ADS! 555-1342
PROFESSIONAL EMPLOYMENT
AUDITION! Seeking young women for exclusive club contract. No prior experience necessary. Competitive rates! Launch your rise to STARDOM! Contact Mr. Braddock at 980 Tower, Gotham City, 555-0302
42ND ST.
"MELODY KNEW THAT WHEN SHE LEFT...
"...SHE JUST DIDN'T KNOW HOW DIFFERENT.
"AND NO, THEY DIDN'T PUT THE NEEDLE IN HER ARM THE LAST TIME...
"...BUT THEY DID THE FIRST.

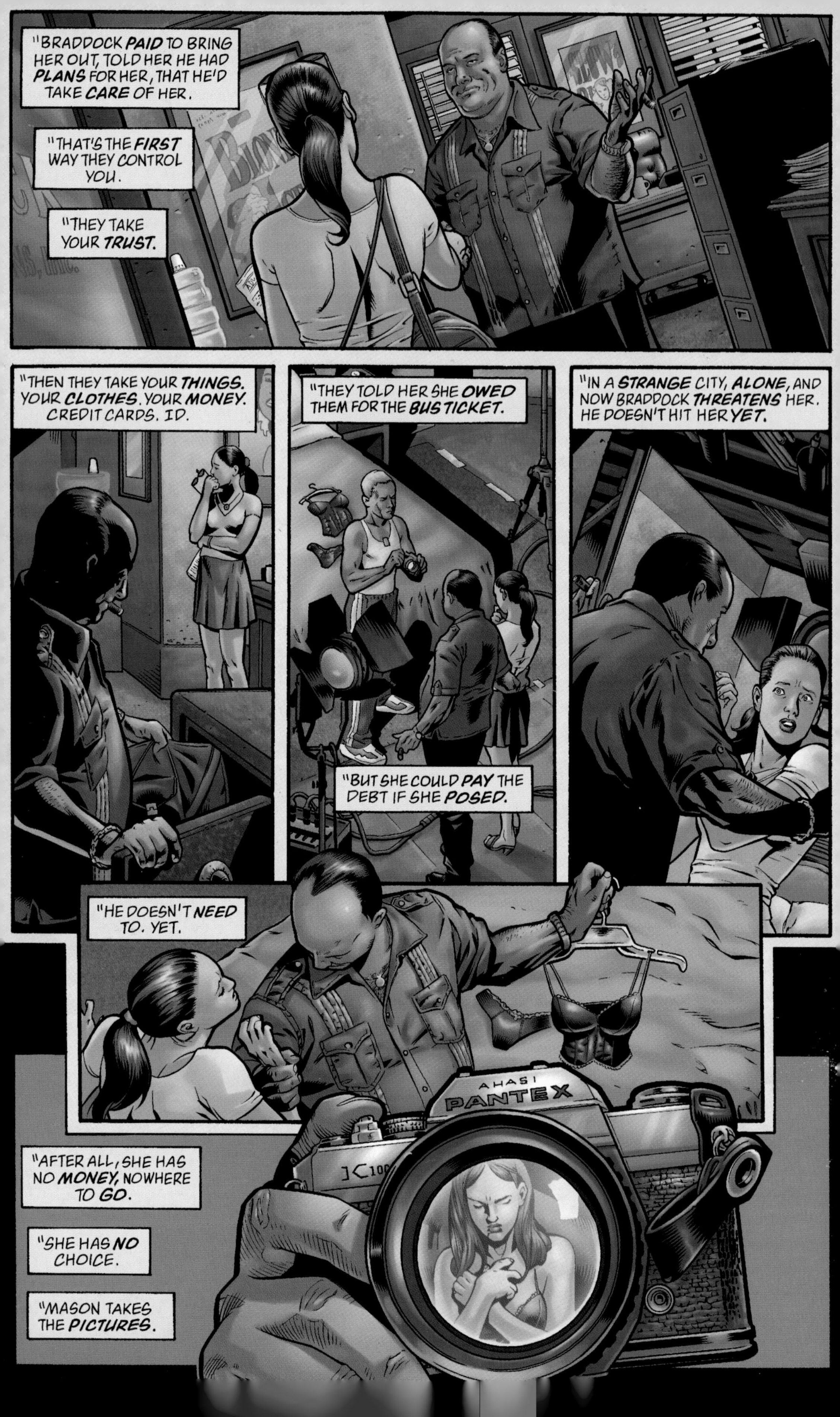
"BRADDOCK PAID TO BRING HER OUT, TOLD HER HE HAD PLANS FOR HER, THAT HE'D TAKE CARE OF HER.
"THAT'S THE FIRST WAY THEY CONTROL YOU.
"THEY TAKE YOUR TRUST.
"THEN THEY TAKE YOUR THINGS. YOUR CLOTHES. YOUR MONEY. CREDIT CARDS. ID.
"THEY TOLD HER SHE OWED THEM FOR THE BUS TICKET.
"BUT SHE COULD PAY THE DEBT IF SHE POSED.
"IN A STRANGE CITY, ALONE, AND NOW BRADDOCK THREATENS HER. HE DOESN'T HIT HER YET.
"HE DOESN'T NEED TO. YET.
AHASI
PANTEX
"AFTER ALL, SHE HAS NO MONEY, NOWHERE TO GO.
"SHE HAS NO CHOICE.
"MASON TAKES THE PICTURES.

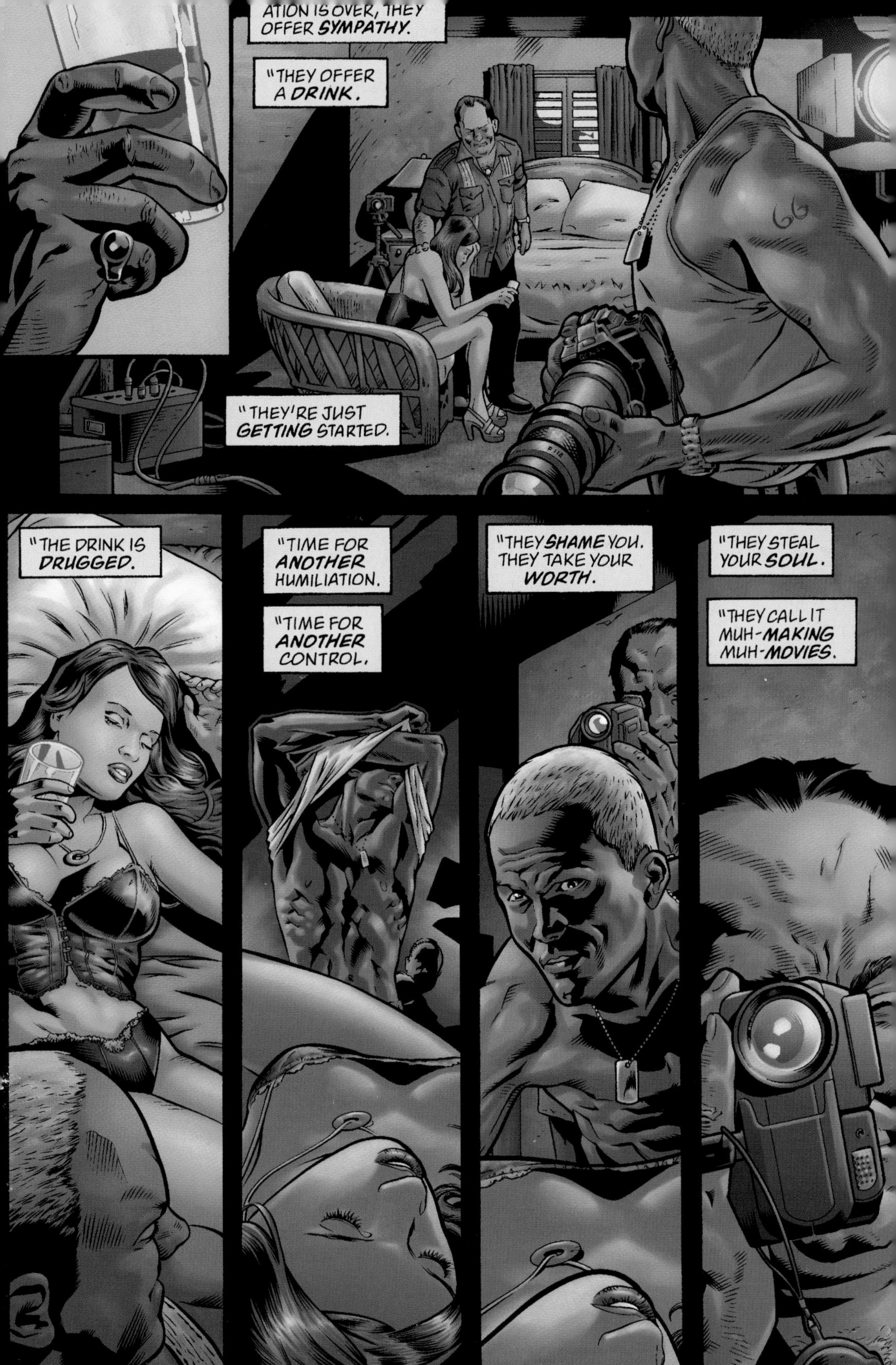
ATION IS OVER, THEY OFFER SYMPATHY.
"THEY OFFER A DRINK.
"THEY'RE JUST GETTING STARTED.
"THE DRINK IS DRUGGED.
"TIME FOR ANOTHER HUMILIATION.
"TIME FOR ANOTHER CONTROL.
"THEY SHAME YOU. THEY TAKE YOUR WORTH.
"THEY STEAL YOUR SOUL.
"THEY CALL IT MUH-MAKING MUH-MOVIES.

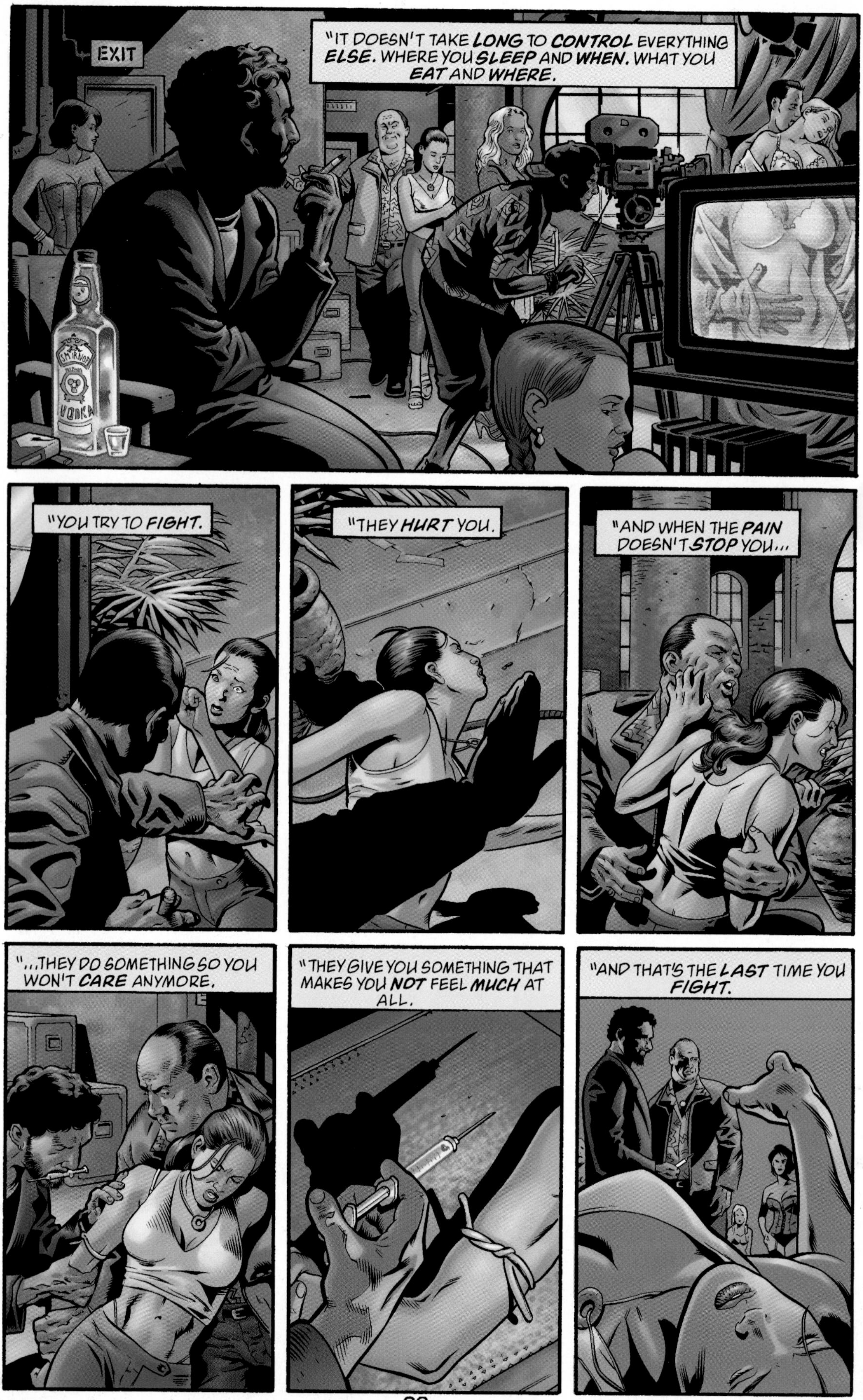
"IT DOESN'T TAKE LONG TO CONTROL EVERYTHING ELSE. WHERE YOU SLEEP AND WHEN. WHAT YOU EAT AND WHERE.
EXIT
VODKA
"YOU TRY TO FIGHT.
"THEY HURT YOU.
"AND WHEN THE PAIN DOESN'T STOP YOU...
"...THEY DO SOMETHING SO YOU WON'T CARE ANYMORE.
"THEY GIVE YOU SOMETHING THAT MAKES YOU NOT FEEL MUCH AT ALL.
"AND THAT'S THE LAST TIME YOU FIGHT.

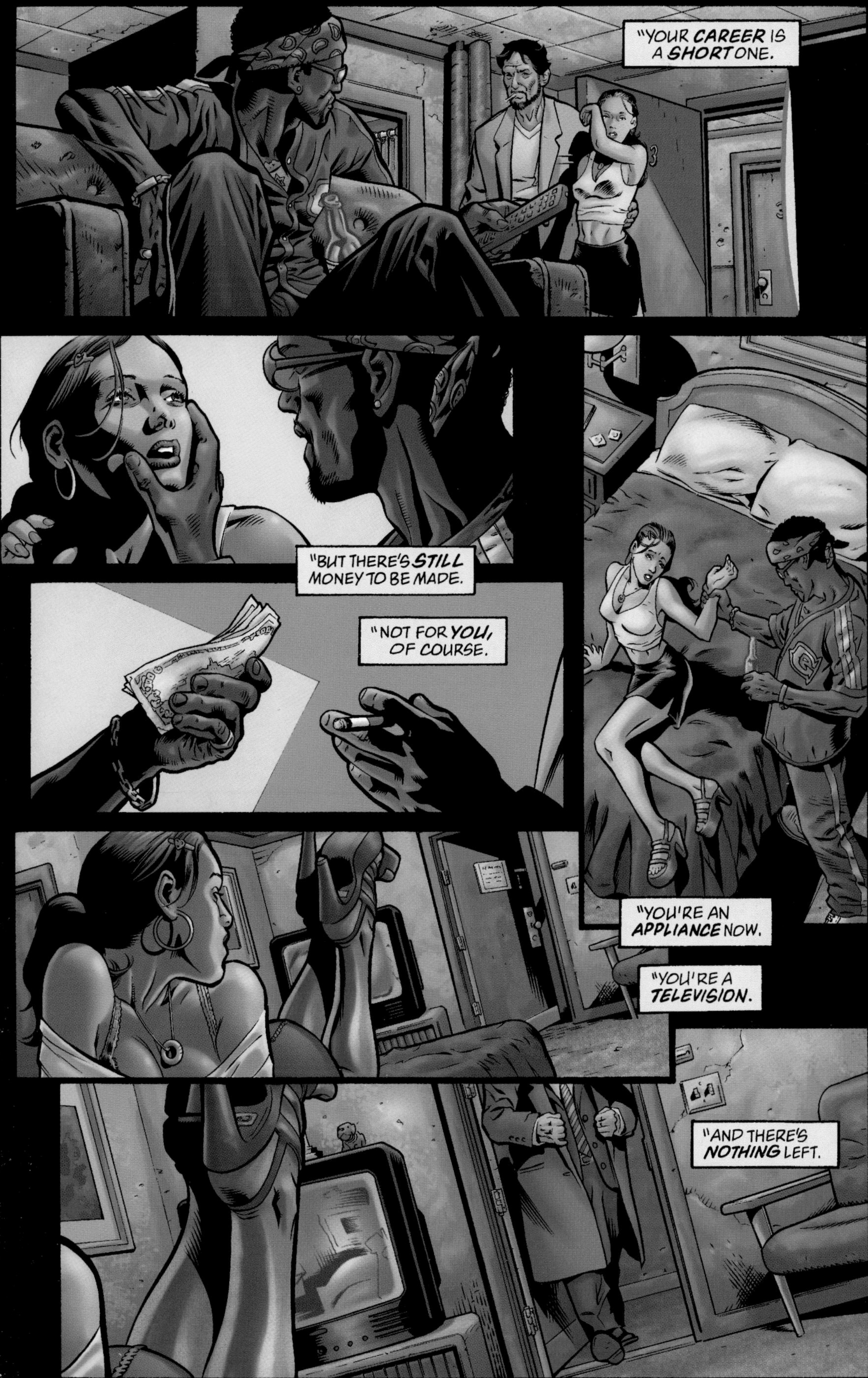
"YOUR CAREER IS A SHORT ONE.
"BUT THERE'S STILL MONEY TO BE MADE.
"NOT FOR YOU, OF COURSE.
"YOU'RE AN APPLIANCE NOW.
"YOU'RE A TELEVISION.
"AND THERE'S NOTHING LEFT.

"AND WHEN YOU *DIE*, COPS MAKE *JOKES*...

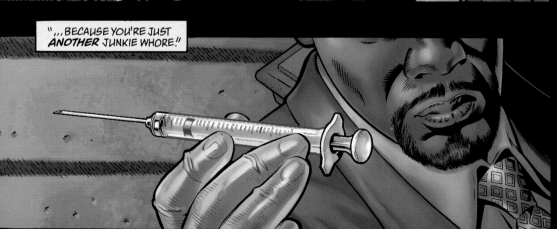

"...BECAUSE YOU'RE JUST *ANOTHER* JUNKIE WHORE."

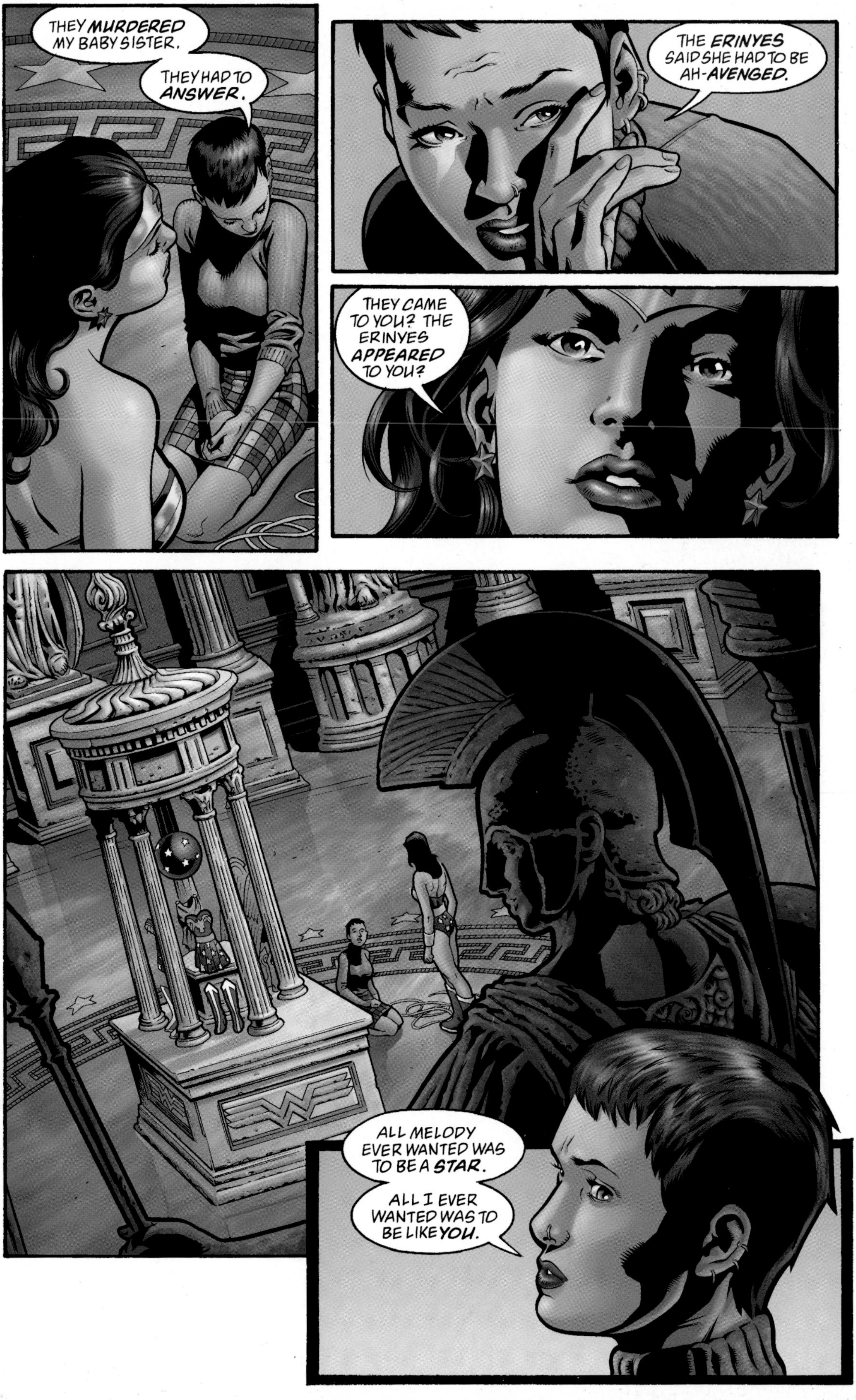
THEY MURDERED MY BABY SISTER.
THEY HAD TO ANSWER.
THE ERINYES SAID SHE HAD TO BE AH-AVENGED.
THEY CAME TO YOU? THE ERINYES APPEARED TO YOU?
ALL MELODY EVER WANTED WAS TO BE A STAR.
ALL I EVER WANTED WAS TO BE LIKE YOU.

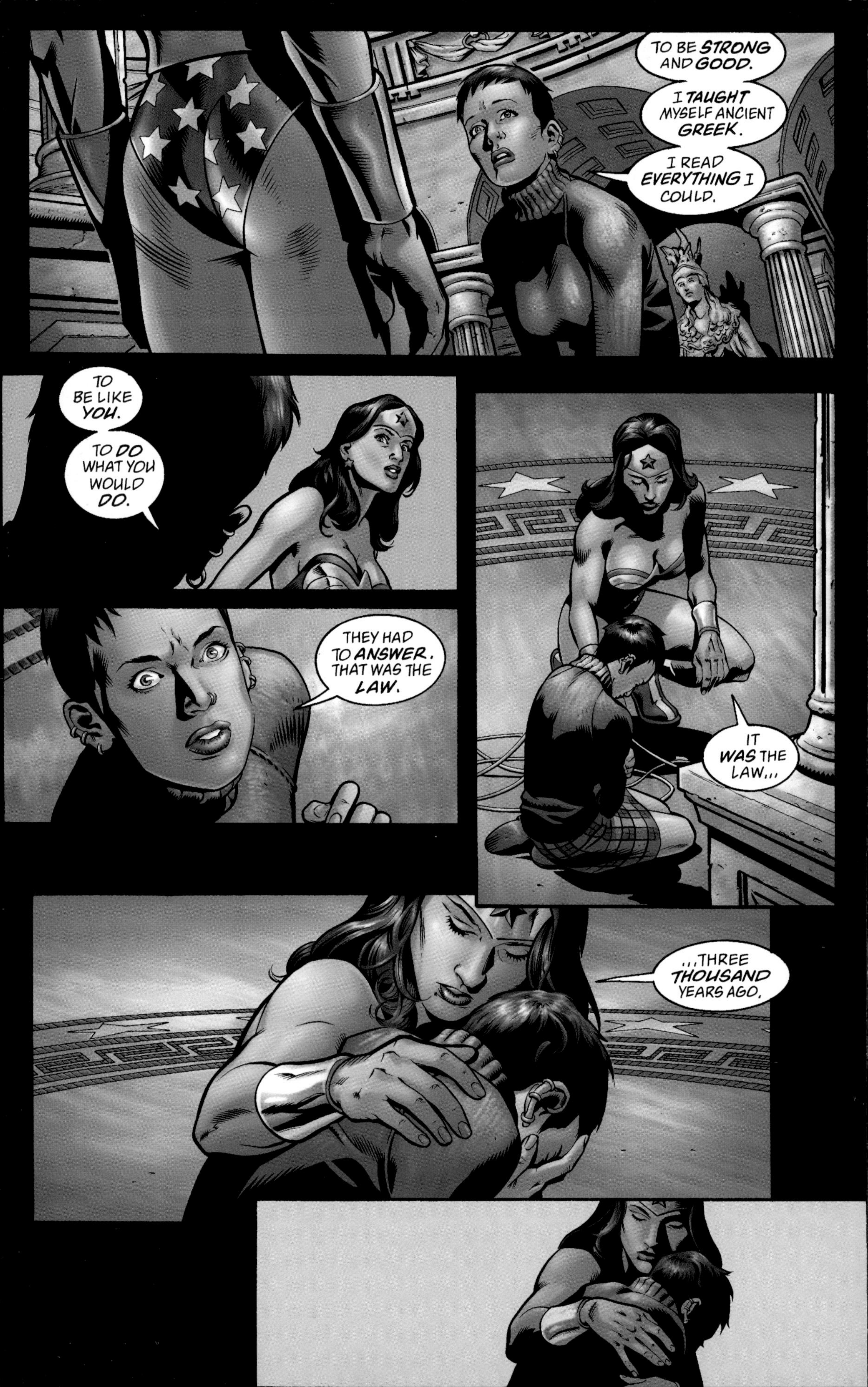
TO BE STRONG AND GOOD.
I TAUGHT MYSELF ANCIENT GREEK.
I READ EVERYTHING I COULD.
TO BE LIKE YOU.
TO DO WHAT YOU WOULD DO.
THEY HAD TO ANSWER. THAT WAS THE LAW.
IT WAS THE LAW...
...THREE THOUSAND YEARS AGO.

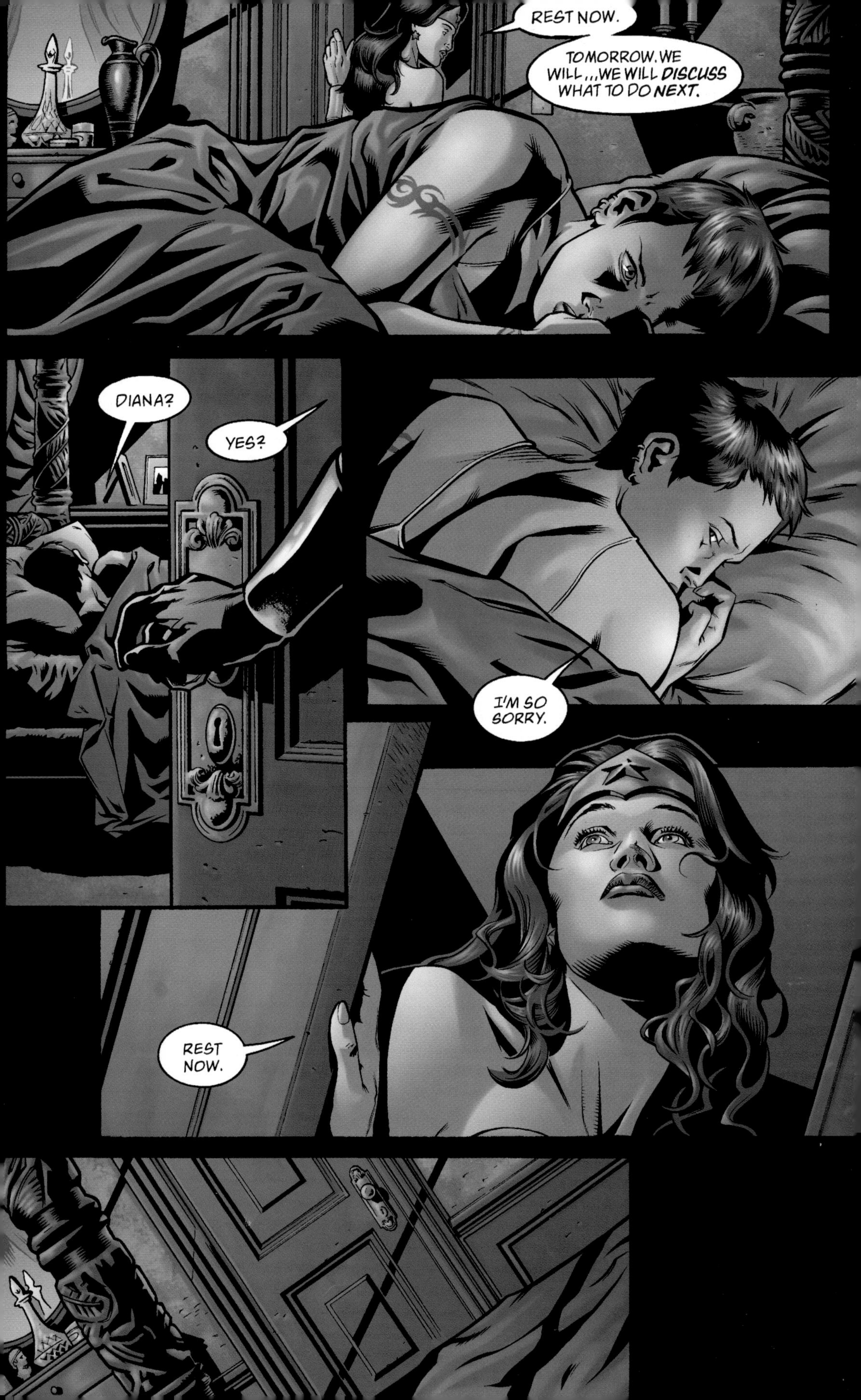
REST NOW.
TOMORROW, WE WILL... WE WILL DISCUSS WHAT TO DO NEXT.
DIANA?
YES?
I'M SO SORRY.
REST NOW.

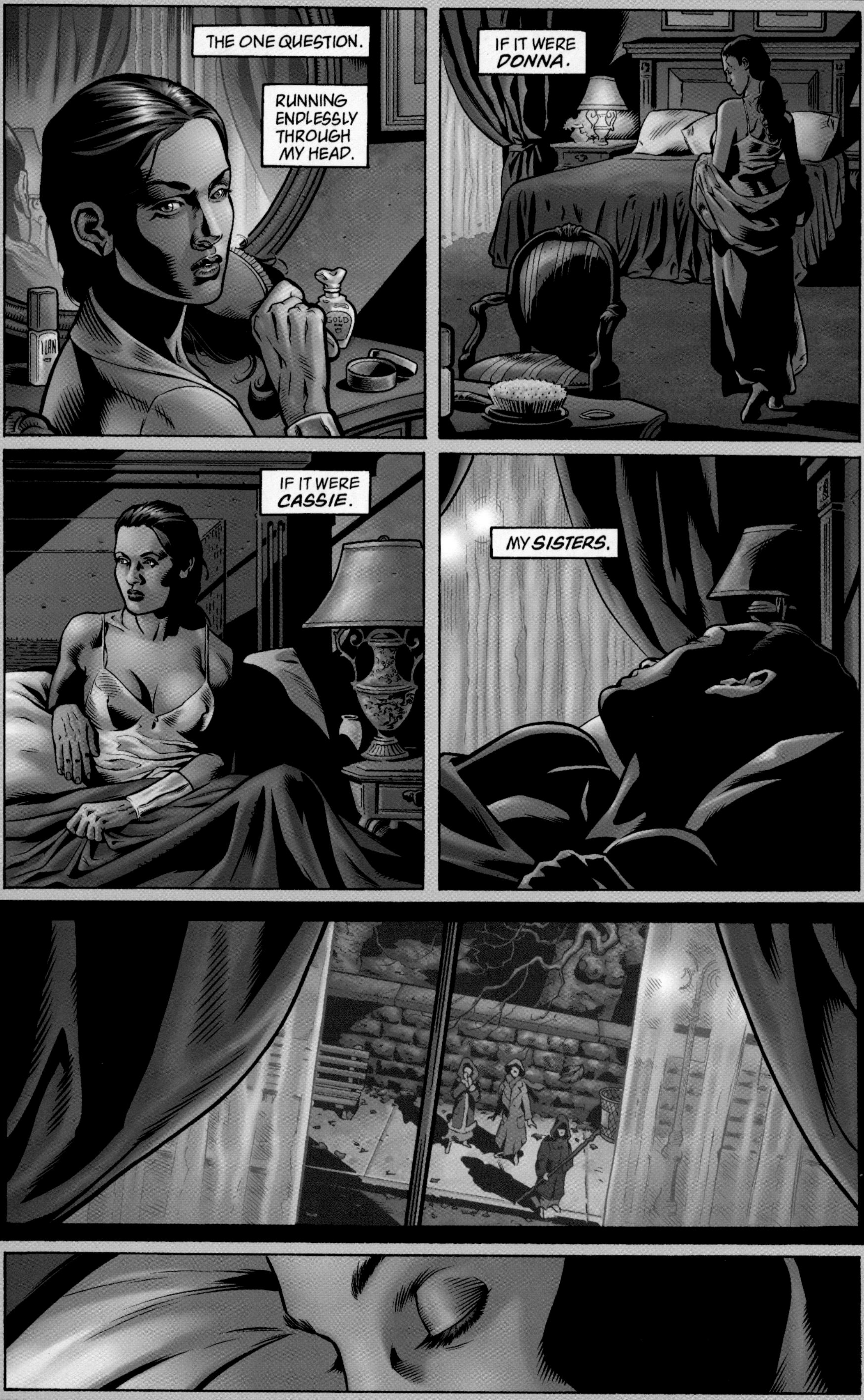
THE ONE QUESTION.
RUNNING ENDLESSLY THROUGH MY HEAD.
IF IT WERE DONNA.
IF IT WERE CASSIE.
MY SISTERS.

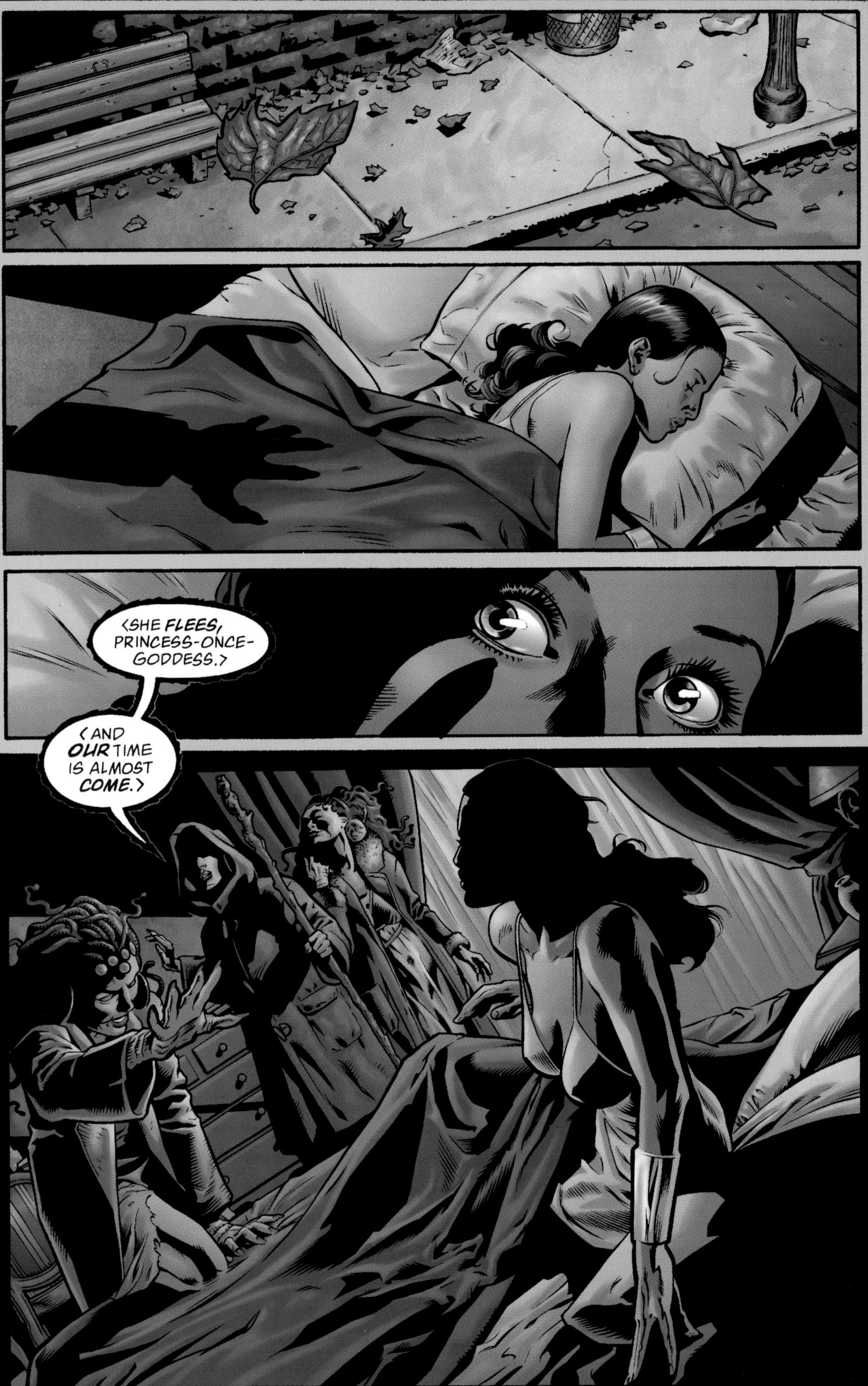
‹SHE **FLEES**, PRINCESS-ONCE-GODDESS.›
‹AND **OUR** TIME IS ALMOST **COME**.›

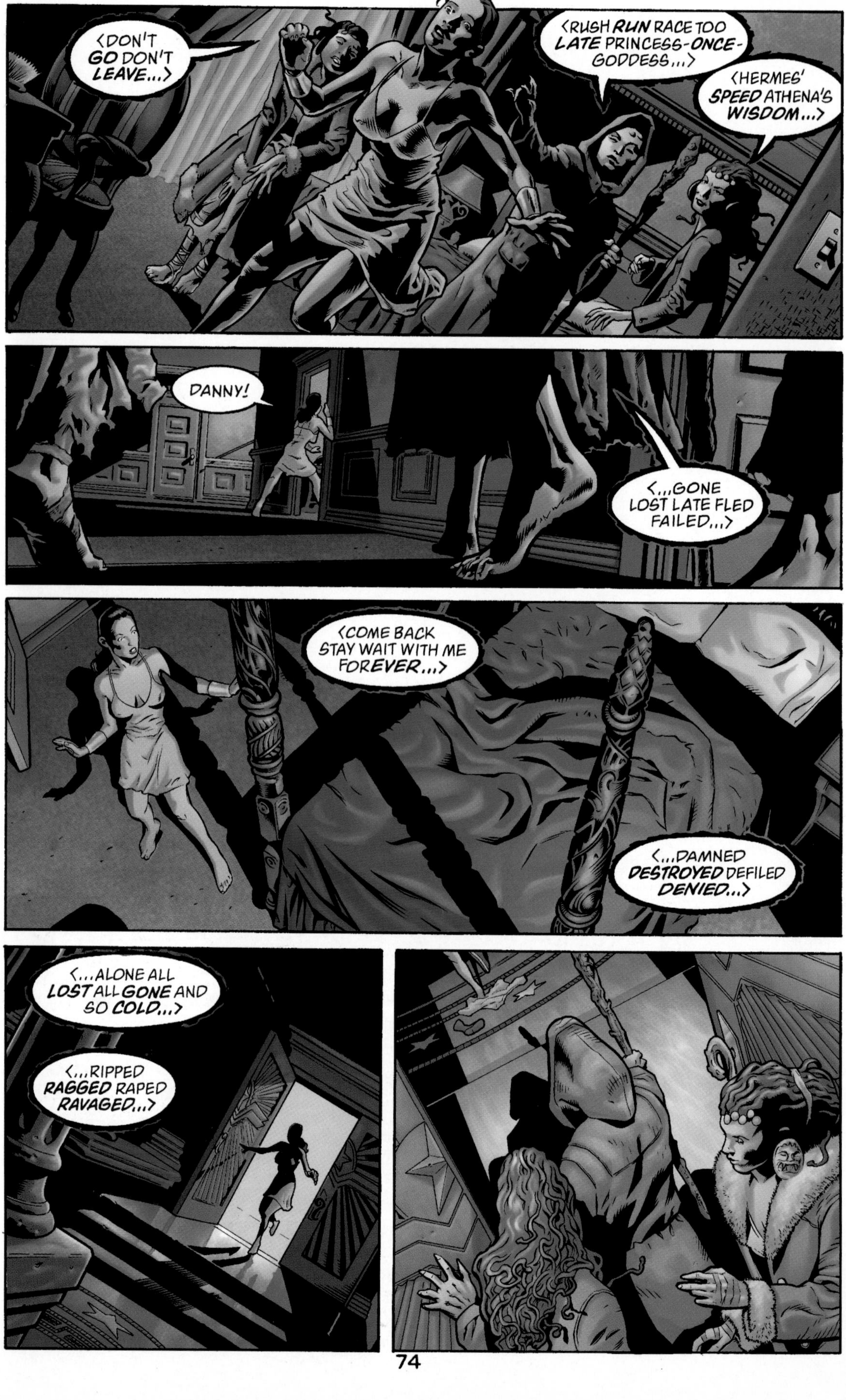

<DON'T GO DON'T LEAVE...>
<RUSH RUN RACE TOO LATE PRINCESS-ONCE-GODDESS...>
<HERMES' SPEED ATHENA'S WISDOM...>
DANNY!
<...GONE LOST LATE FLED FAILED...>
<COME BACK STAY WAIT WITH ME FOREVER...>
<...DAMNED DESTROYED DEFILED DENIED...>
<...ALONE ALL LOST ALL GONE AND SO COLD...>
<...RIPPED RAGGED RAPED RAVAGED...>

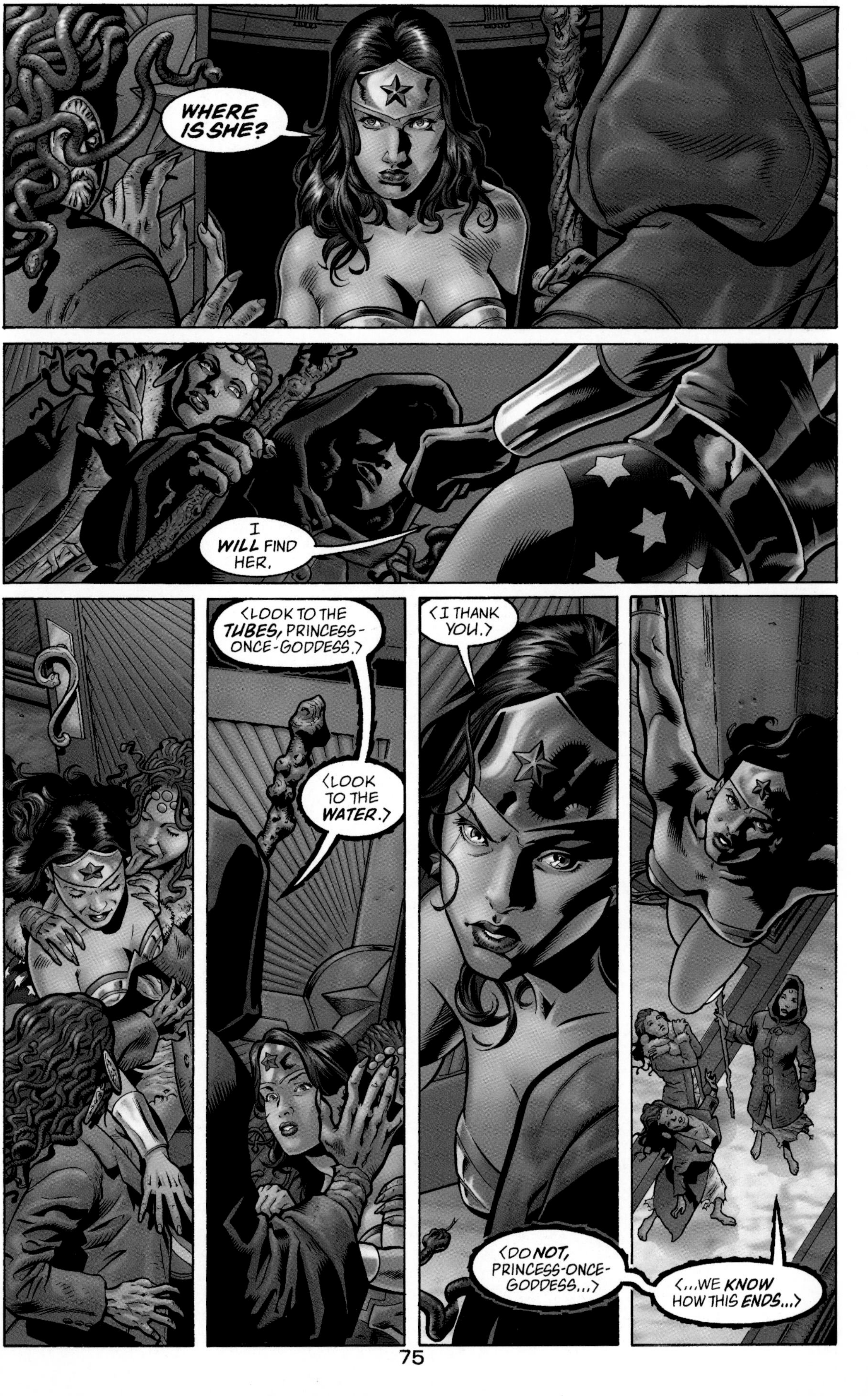
WHERE IS SHE?
I WILL FIND HER.
<LOOK TO THE TUBES, PRINCESS-ONCE-GODDESS.>
<LOOK TO THE WATER.>
<I THANK YOU.>
<DO NOT, PRINCESS-ONCE-GODDESS...>
<...WE KNOW HOW THIS ENDS...>

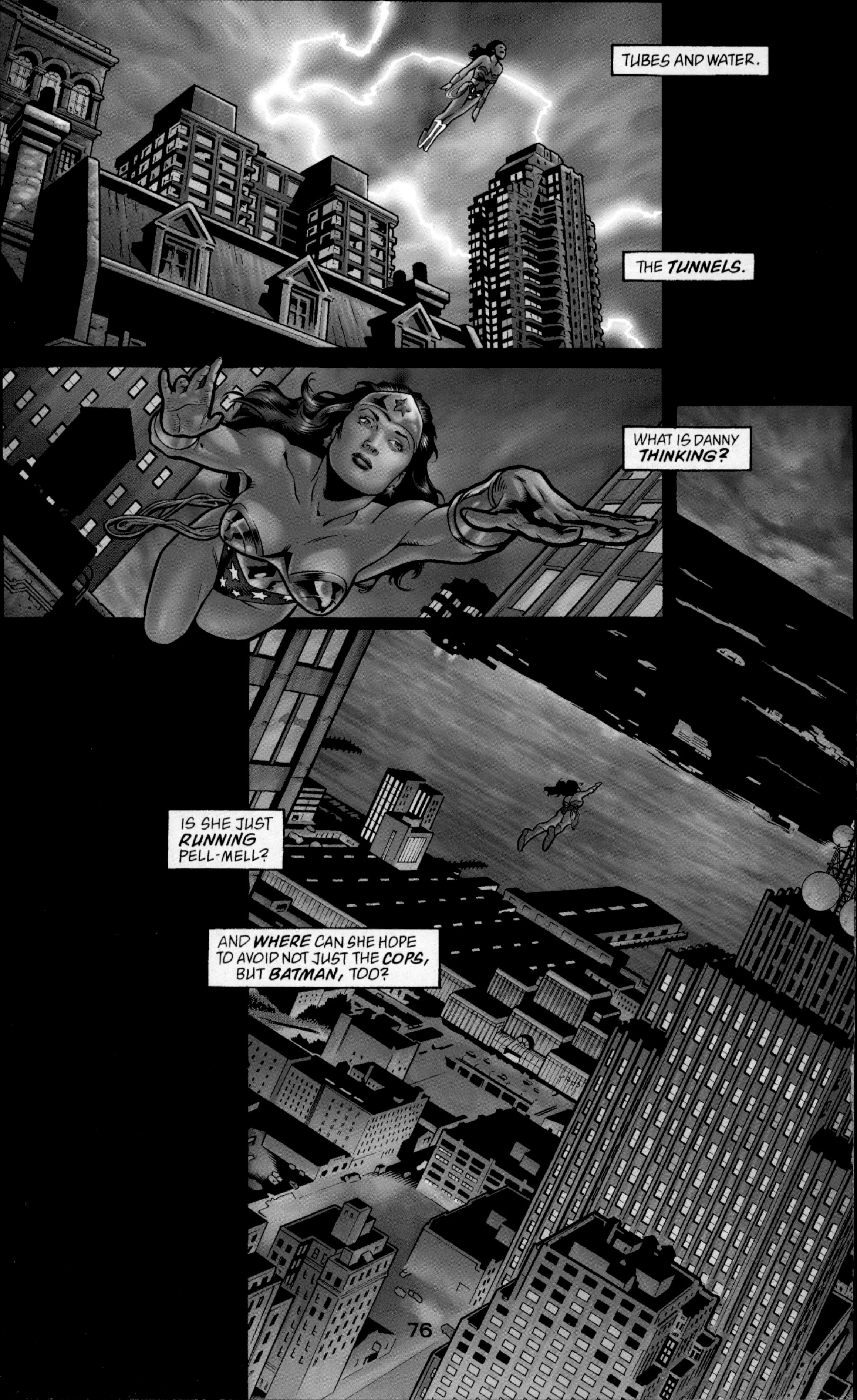
TUBES AND WATER.
THE TUNNELS.
WHAT IS DANNY THINKING?
IS SHE JUST RUNNING PELL-MELL?
AND WHERE CAN SHE HOPE TO AVOID NOT JUST THE COPS, BUT BATMAN, TOO?

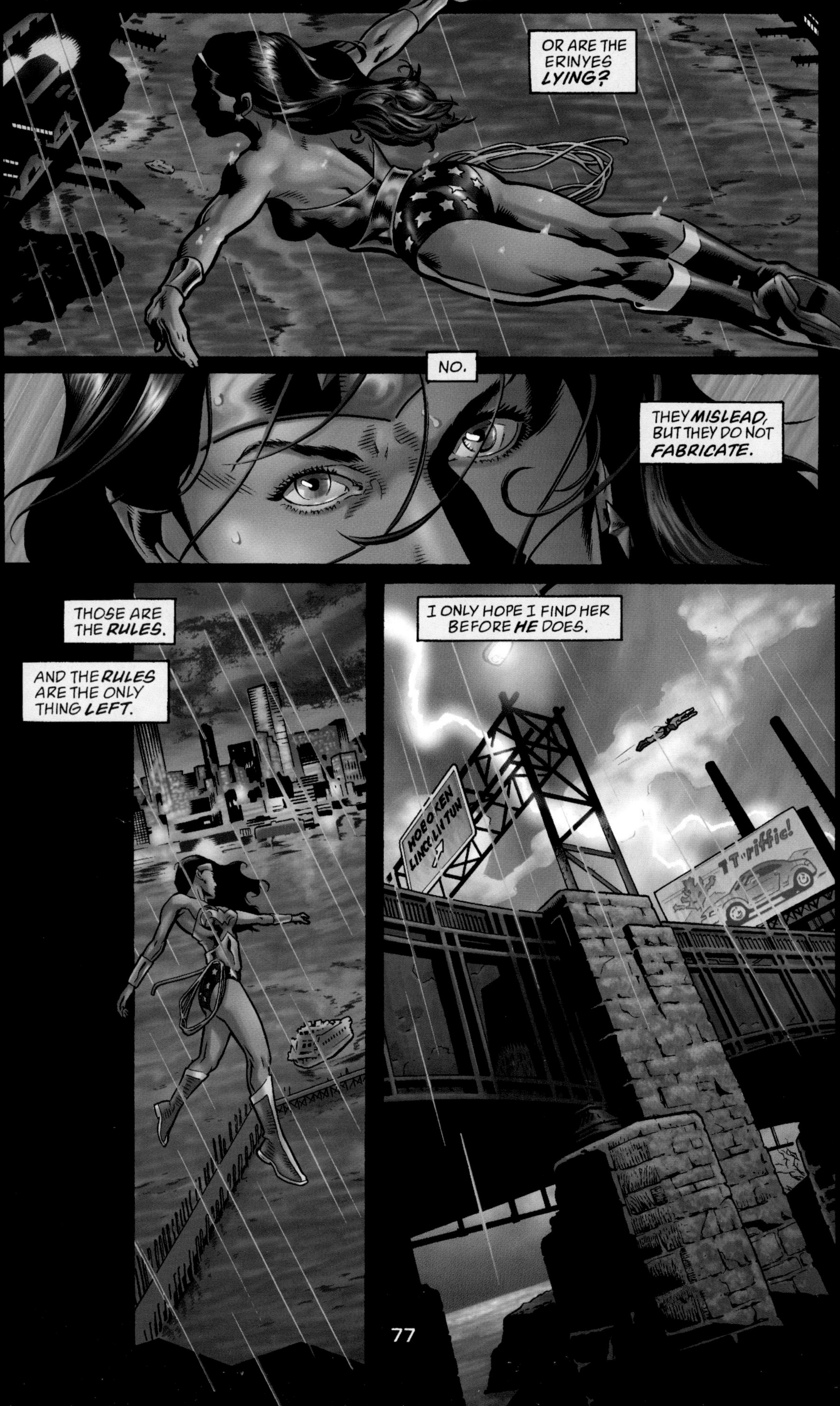
OR ARE THE ERINYES LYING?
NO.
THEY MISLEAD, BUT THEY DO NOT FABRICATE.
THOSE ARE THE RULES.
AND THE RULES ARE THE ONLY THING LEFT.
I ONLY HOPE I FIND HER BEFORE HE DOES.

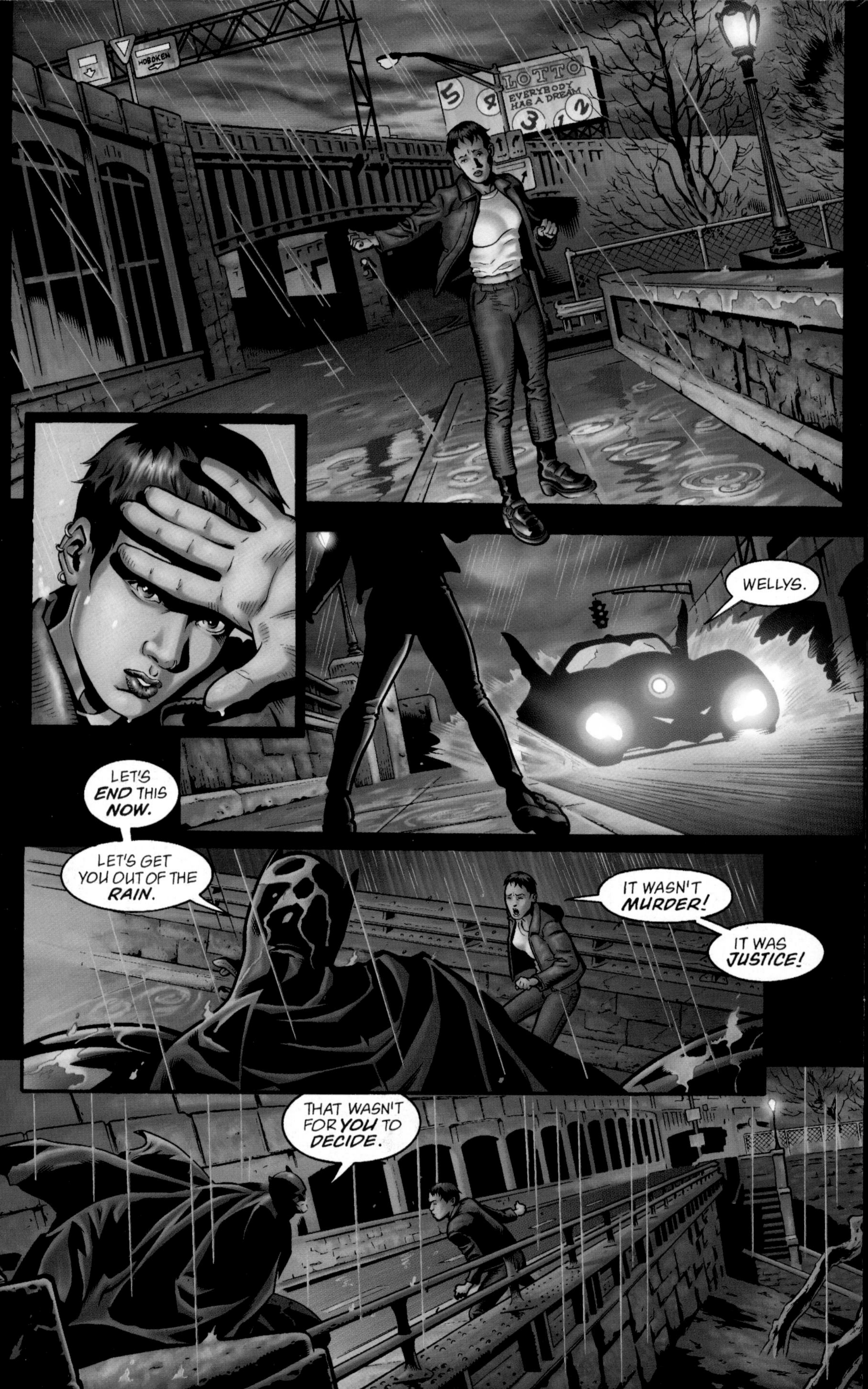
HOBOKEN
LOTTO
EVERYBODY HAS A DREAM
WELLYS.
LET'S END THIS NOW.
LET'S GET YOU OUT OF THE RAIN.
IT WASN'T MURDER!
IT WAS JUSTICE!
THAT WASN'T FOR YOU TO DECIDE.

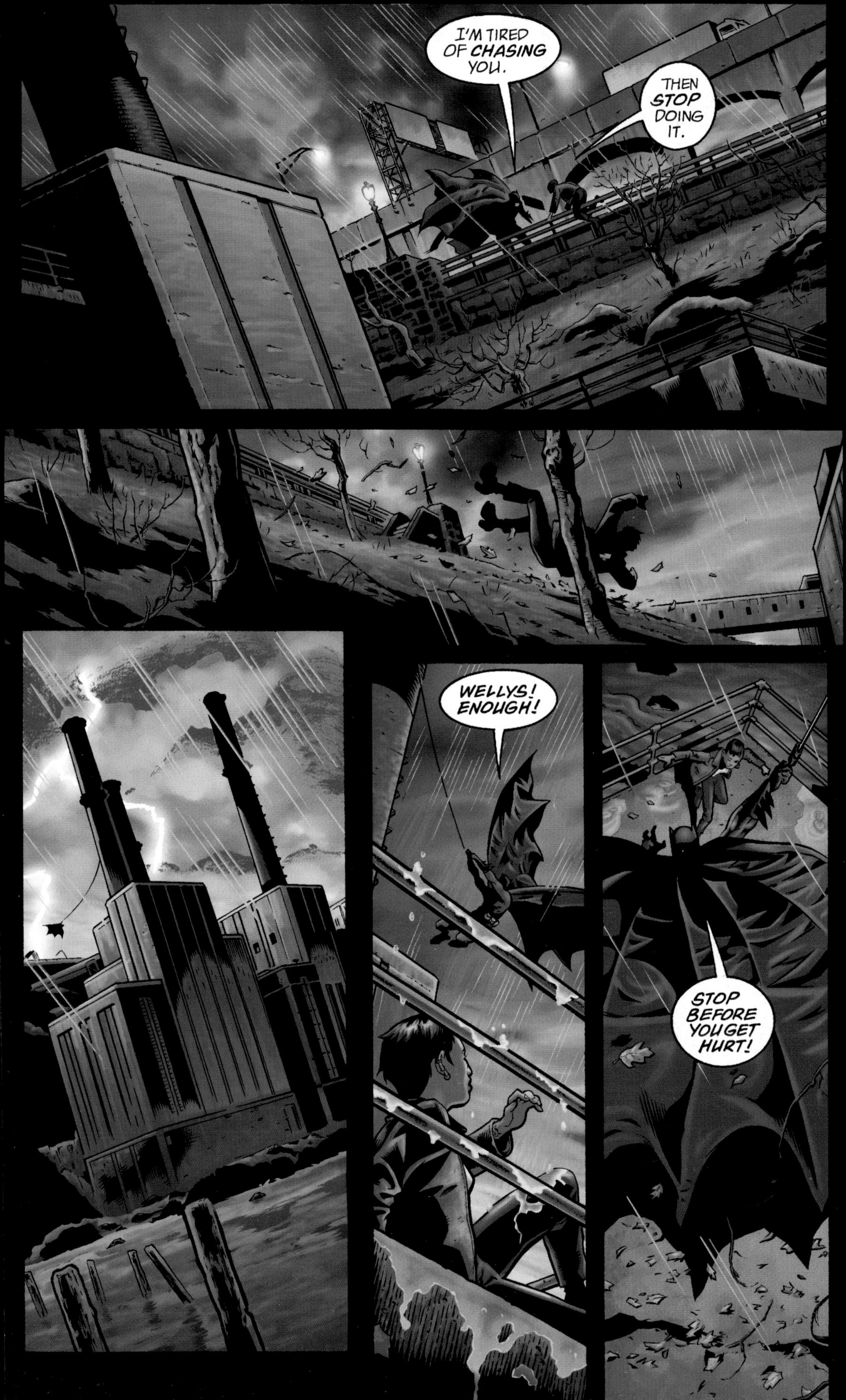
I'M TIRED OF CHASING YOU.
THEN STOP DOING IT.
WELLYS! ENOUGH!
STOP BEFORE YOU GET HURT!

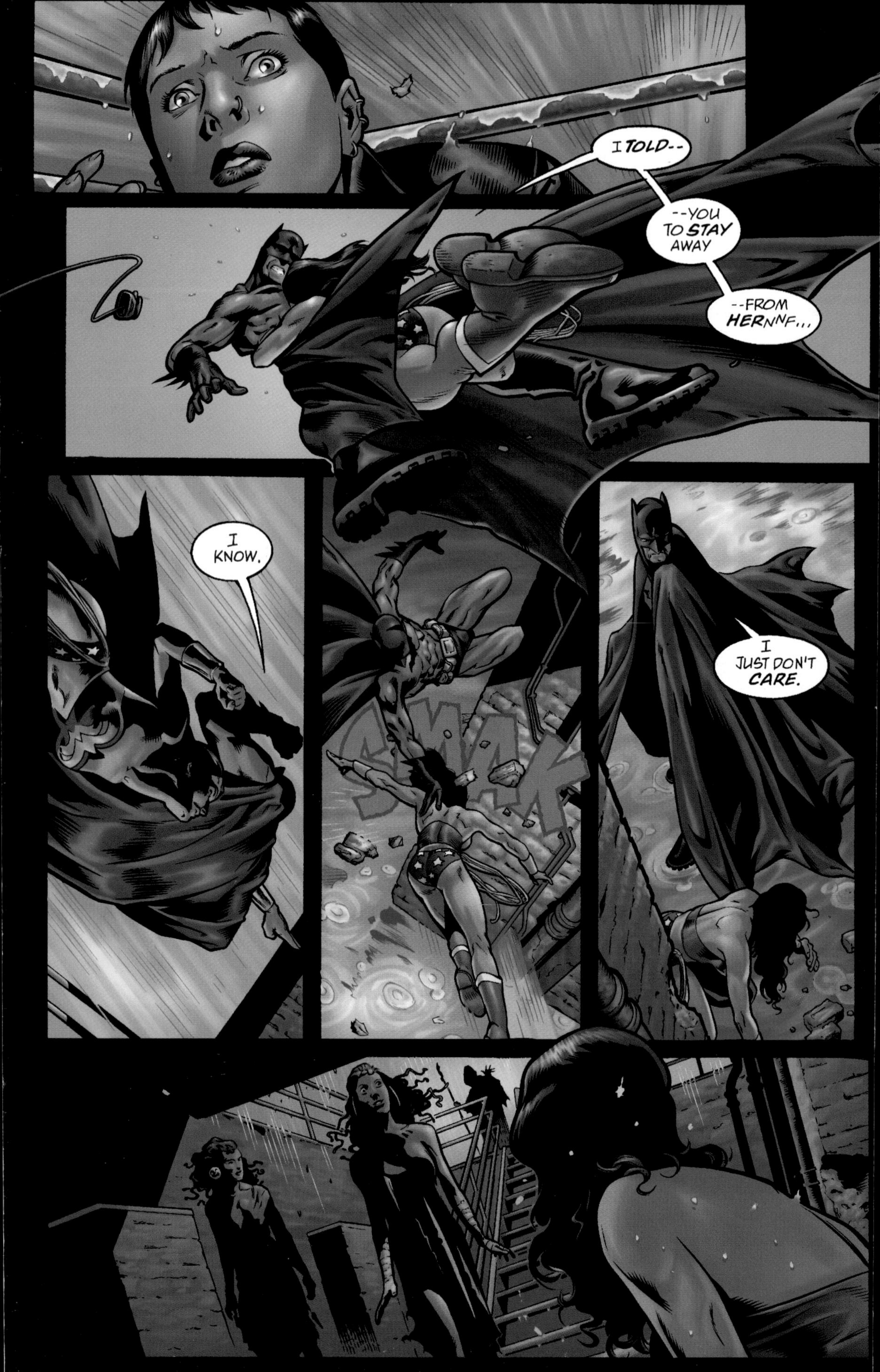
I TOLD--
--YOU TO STAY AWAY
--FROM HERNNF...
I KNOW.
SMAK
I JUST DON'T CARE.

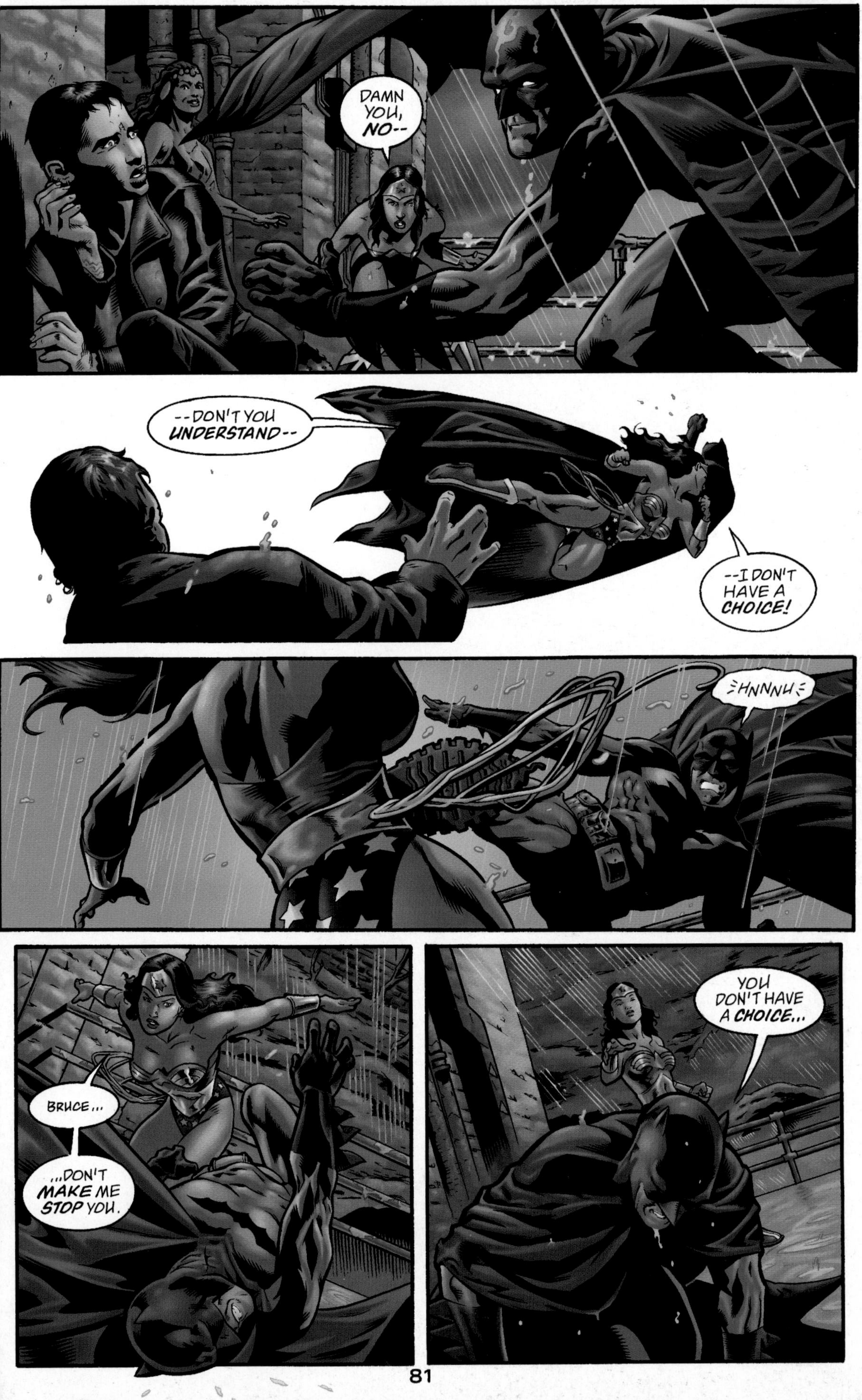
DAMN YOU, NO--
--DON'T YOU UNDERSTAND--
--I DON'T HAVE A CHOICE!
HNNNU
BRUCE...
...DON'T MAKE ME STOP YOU.
YOU DON'T HAVE A CHOICE...

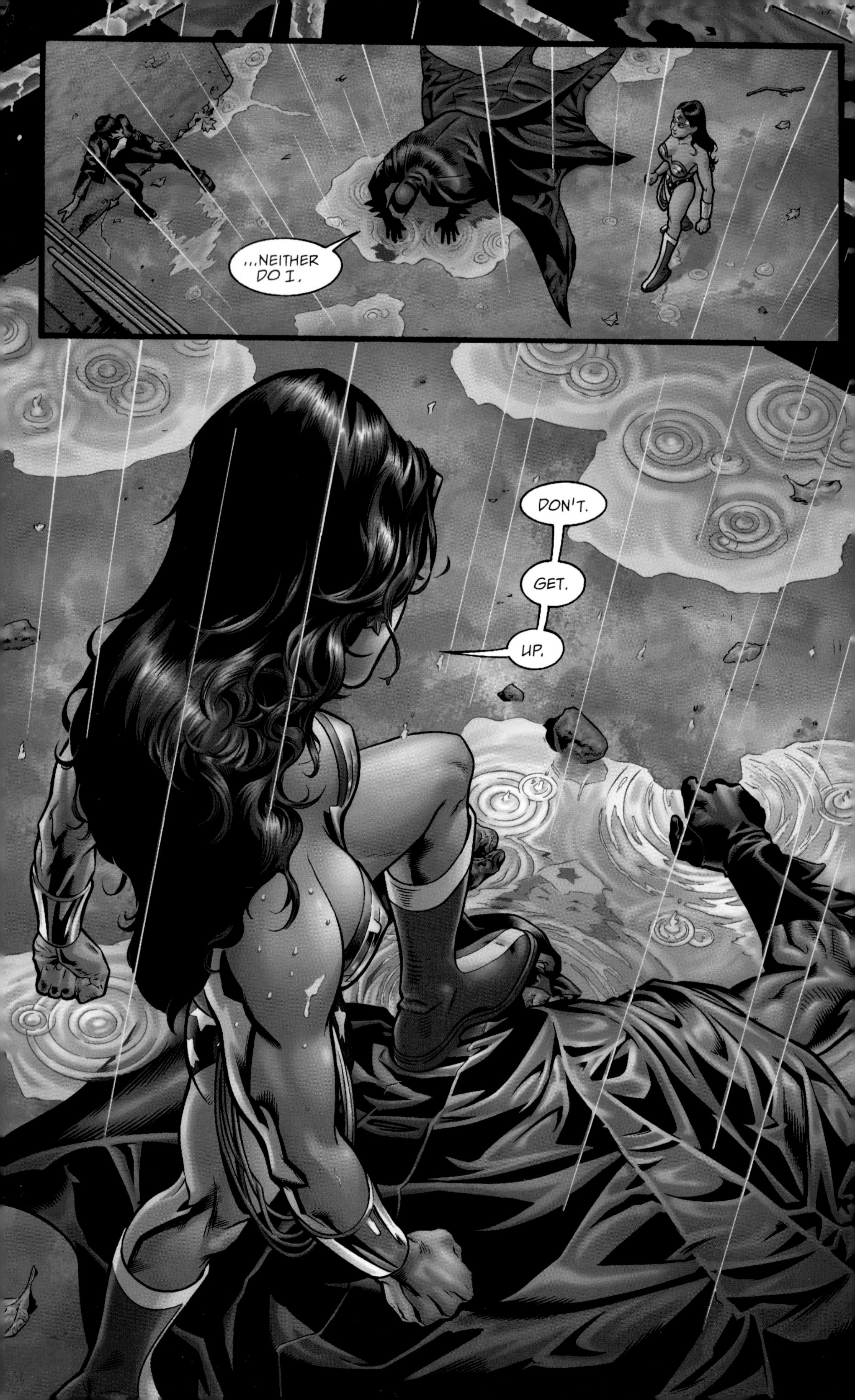
...NEITHER DO I.
DON'T.
GET.
UP.

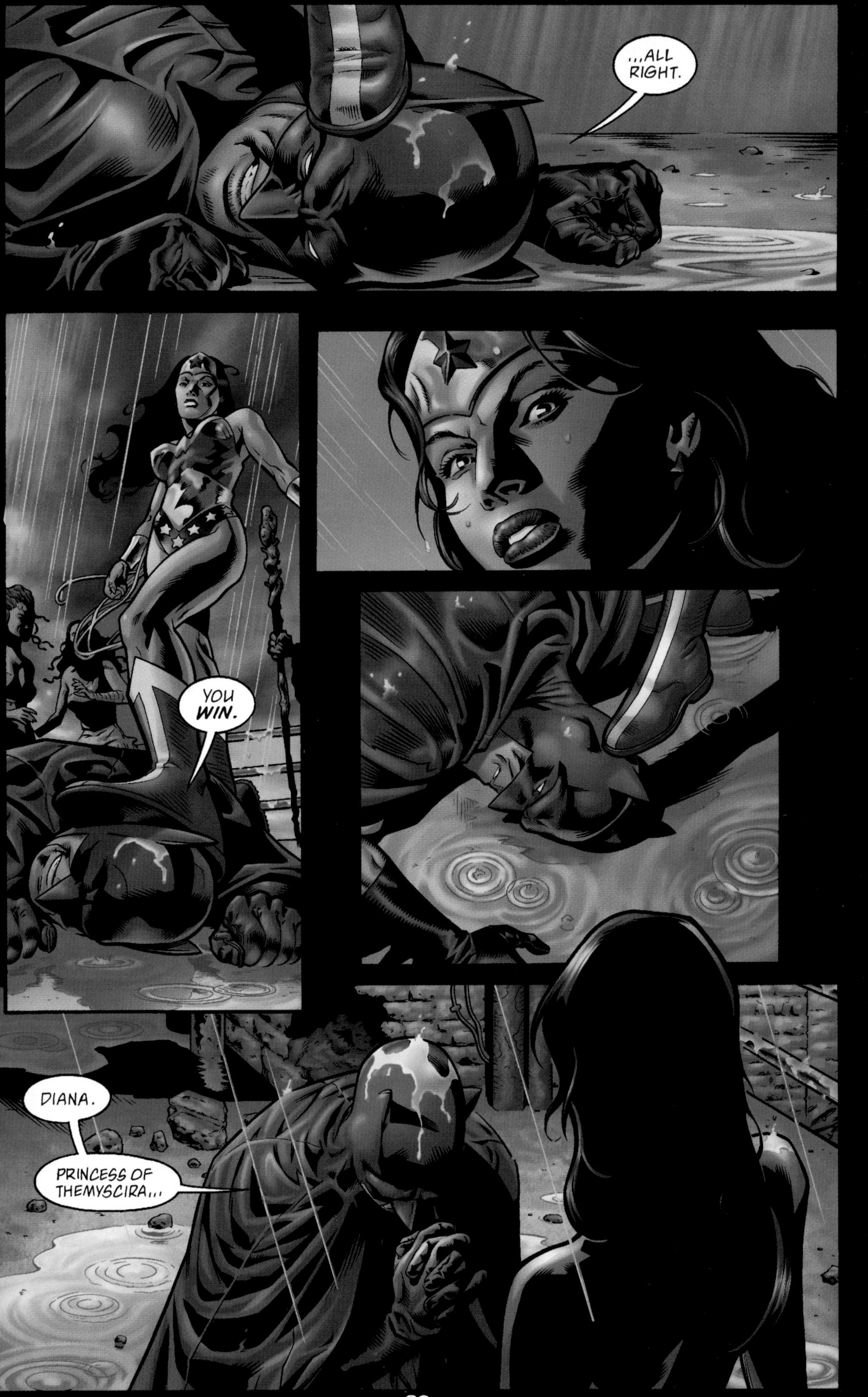
...ALL RIGHT.
YOU WIN.
DIANA.
PRINCESS OF THEMYSCIRA...

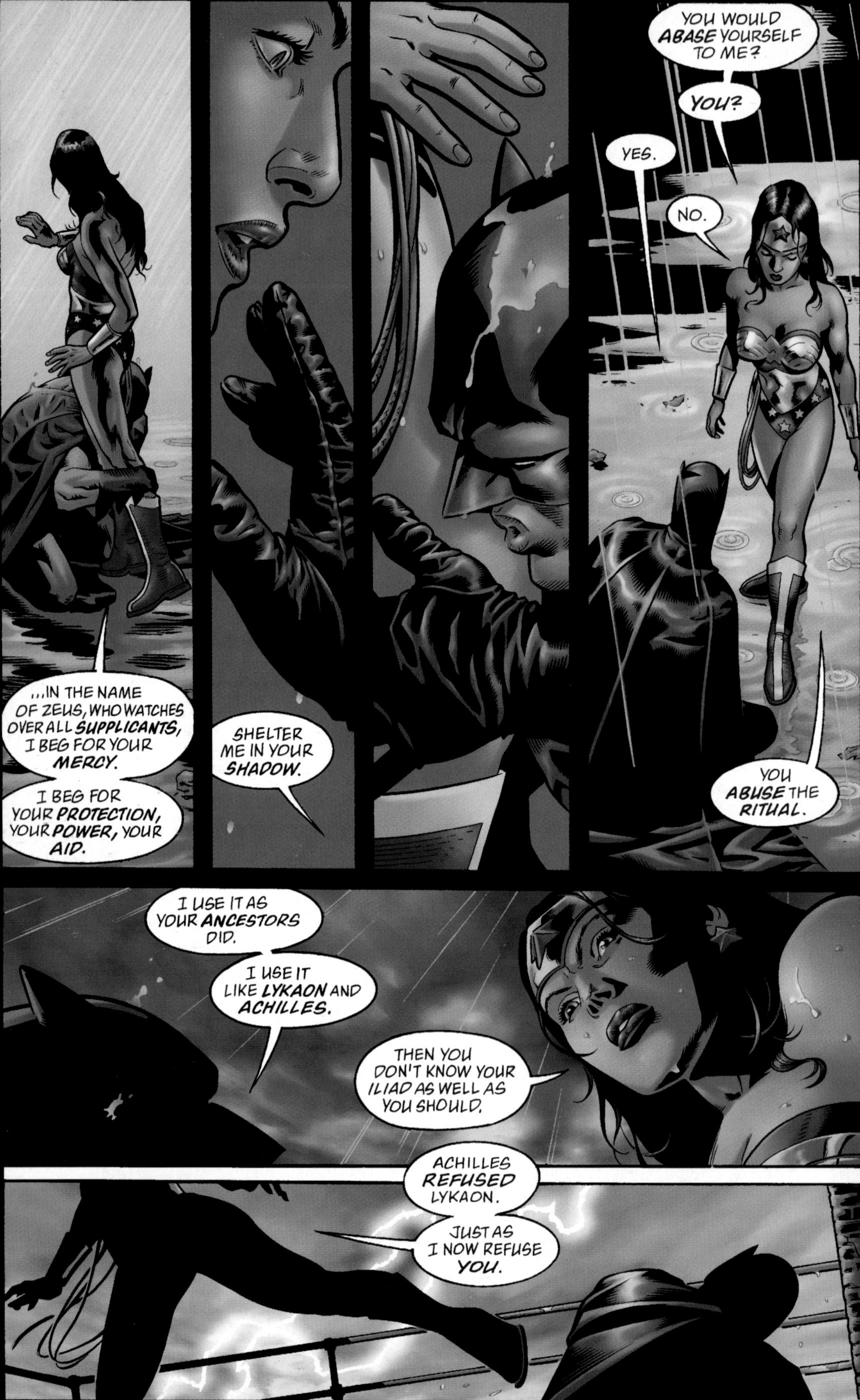
...IN THE NAME OF ZEUS, WHO WATCHES OVER ALL SUPPLICANTS, I BEG FOR YOUR MERCY.
I BEG FOR YOUR PROTECTION, YOUR POWER, YOUR AID.
SHELTER ME IN YOUR SHADOW.
YOU WOULD ABASE YOURSELF TO ME?
YOU?
YES.
NO.
YOU ABUSE THE RITUAL.
I USE IT AS YOUR ANCESTORS DID.
I USE IT LIKE LYKAON AND ACHILLES.
THEN YOU DON'T KNOW YOUR ILIAD AS WELL AS YOU SHOULD.
ACHILLES REFUSED LYKAON.
JUST AS I NOW REFUSE YOU.

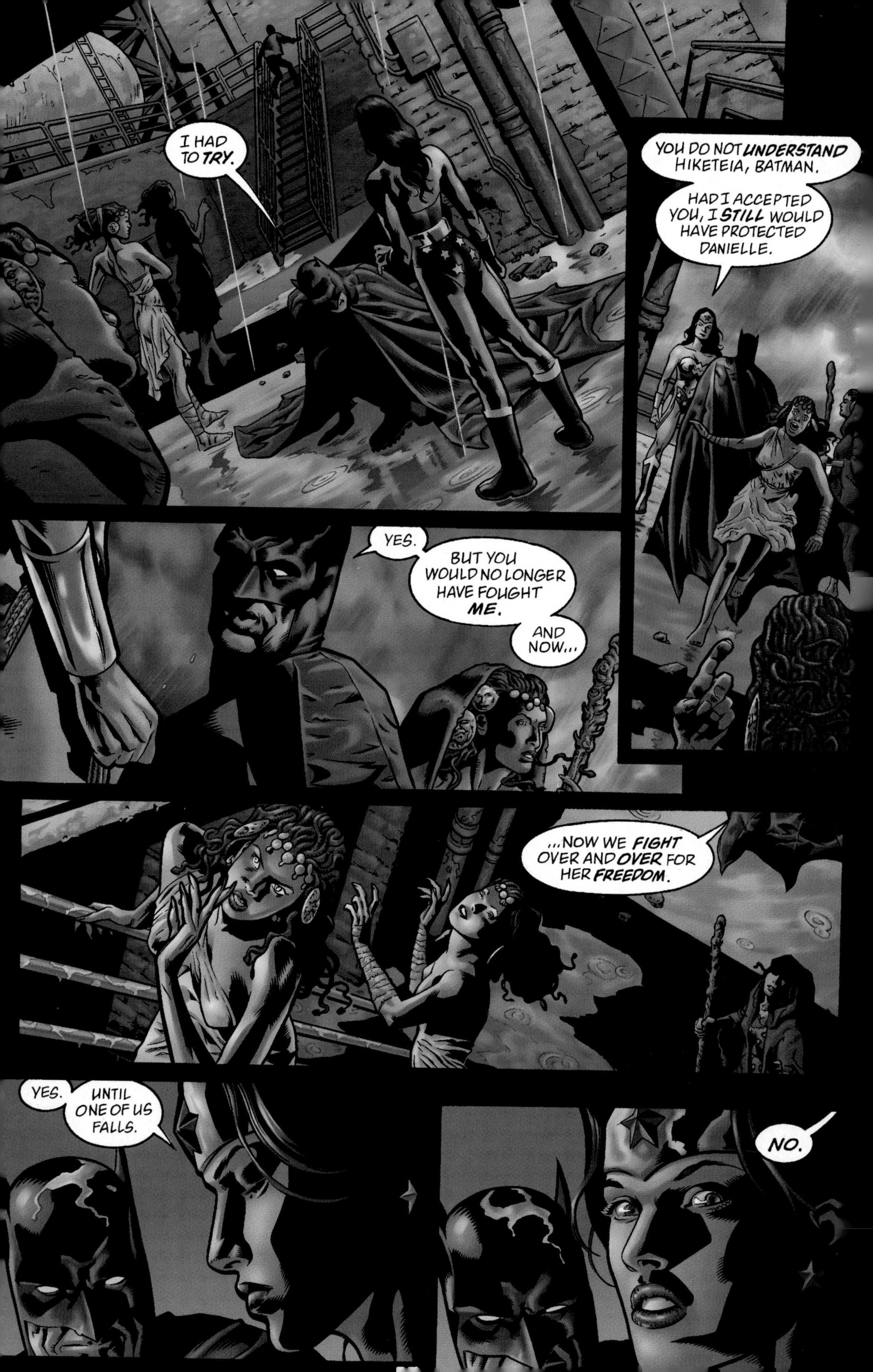
I HAD TO TRY.
YOU DO NOT UNDERSTAND HIKETEIA, BATMAN.
HAD I ACCEPTED YOU, I STILL WOULD HAVE PROTECTED DANIELLE.
YES.
BUT YOU WOULD NO LONGER HAVE FOUGHT ME.
AND NOW...
...NOW WE FIGHT OVER AND OVER FOR HER FREEDOM.
YES.
UNTIL ONE OF US FALLS.
NO.

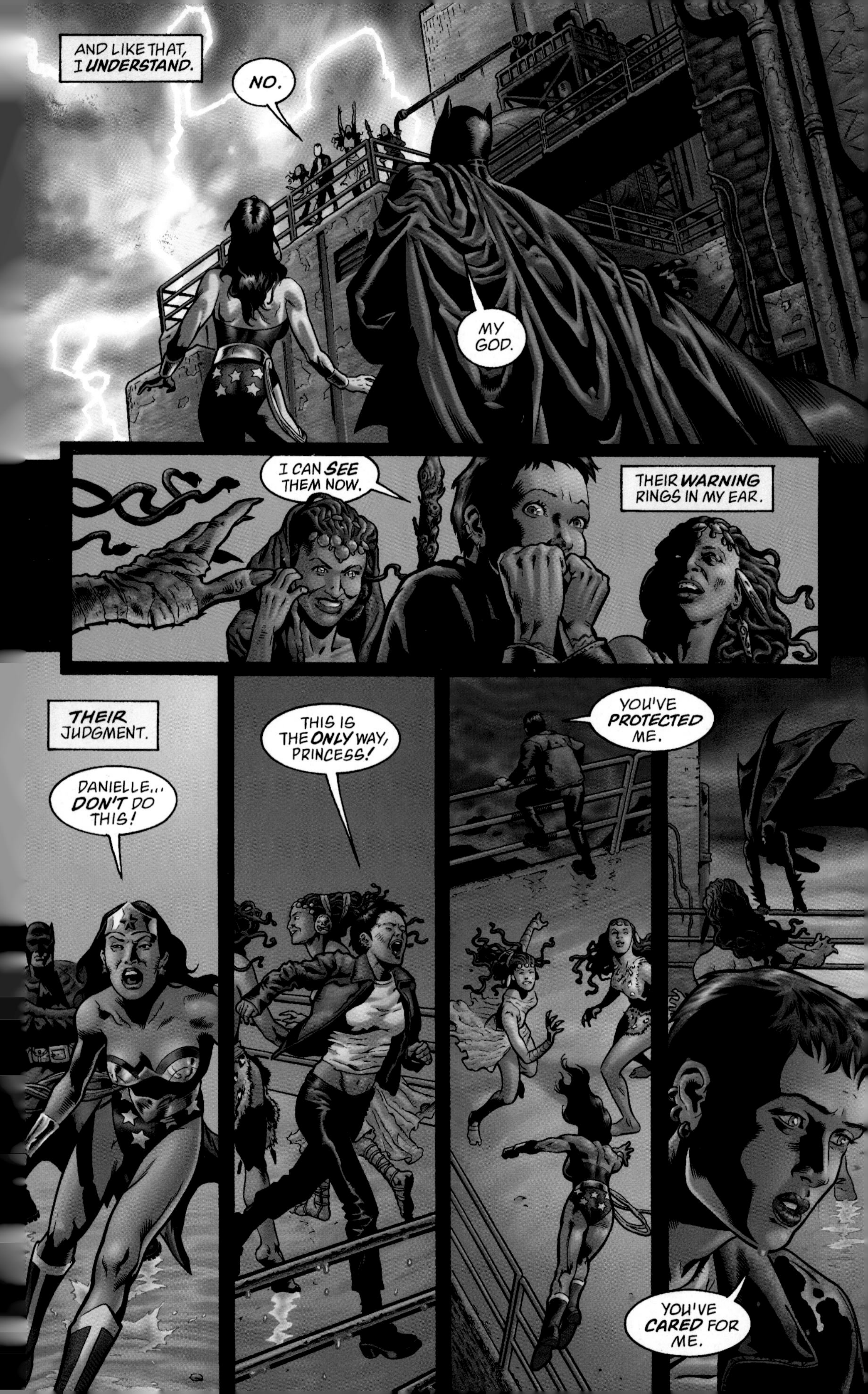
AND LIKE THAT, I UNDERSTAND.
NO.
MY GOD.
I CAN SEE THEM NOW.
THEIR WARNING RINGS IN MY EAR.
THEIR JUDGMENT.
DANIELLE... DON'T DO THIS!
THIS IS THE ONLY WAY, PRINCESS!
YOU'VE PROTECTED ME.
YOU'VE CARED FOR ME.

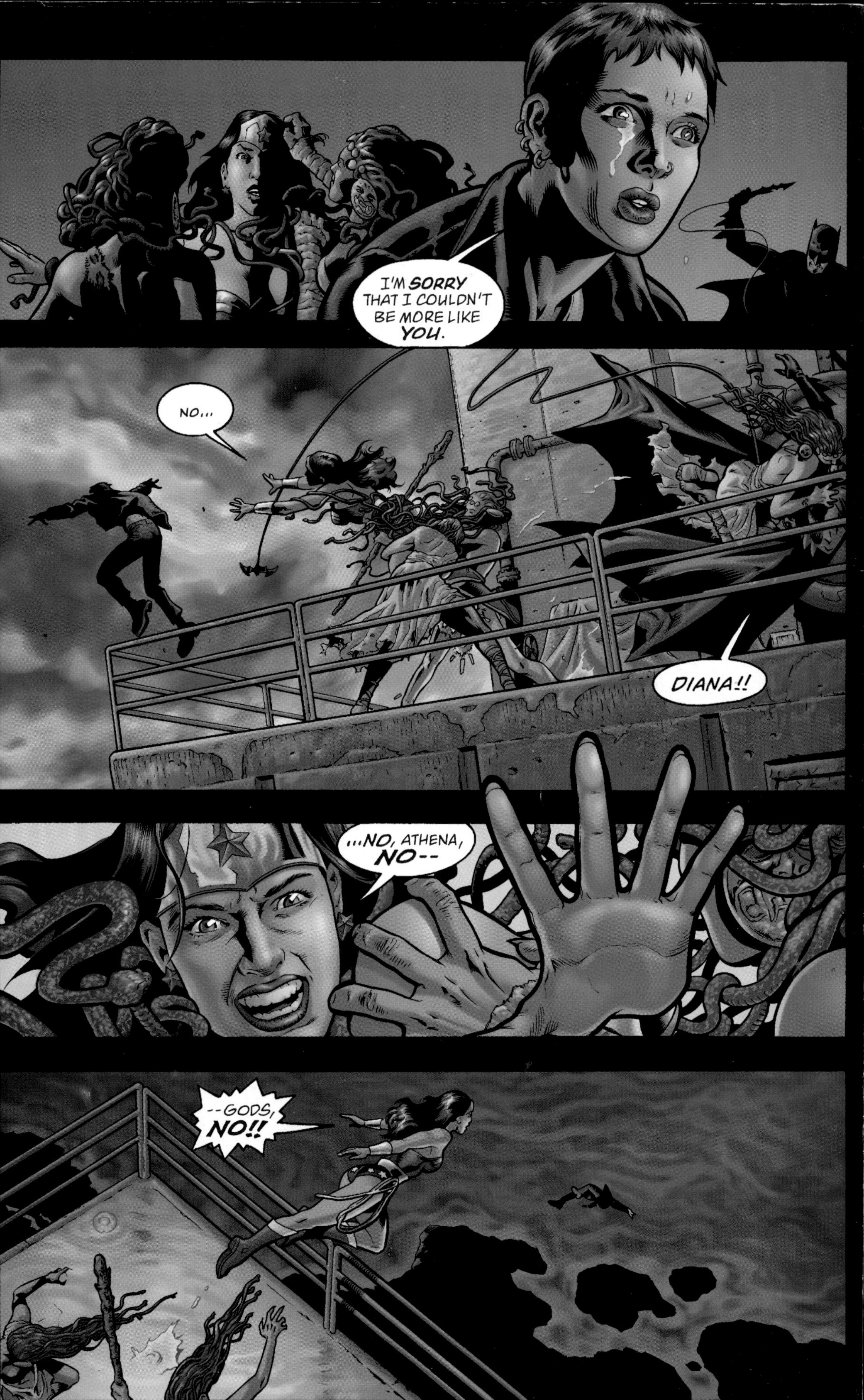
I'M SORRY THAT I COULDN'T BE MORE LIKE YOU.
NO...
DIANA!!
...NO, ATHENA, NO--
--GODS, NO!!

THEIR *LAUGHTER* CHASES ME ALL THE WAY *DOWN...*

...*LAUGHTER* THAT DRIVES *MORTALS* INSANE...

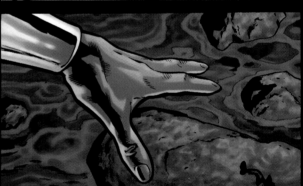

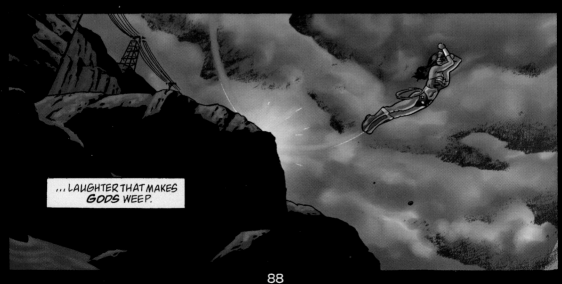

...*LAUGHTER* THAT MAKES *GODS* WEEP.

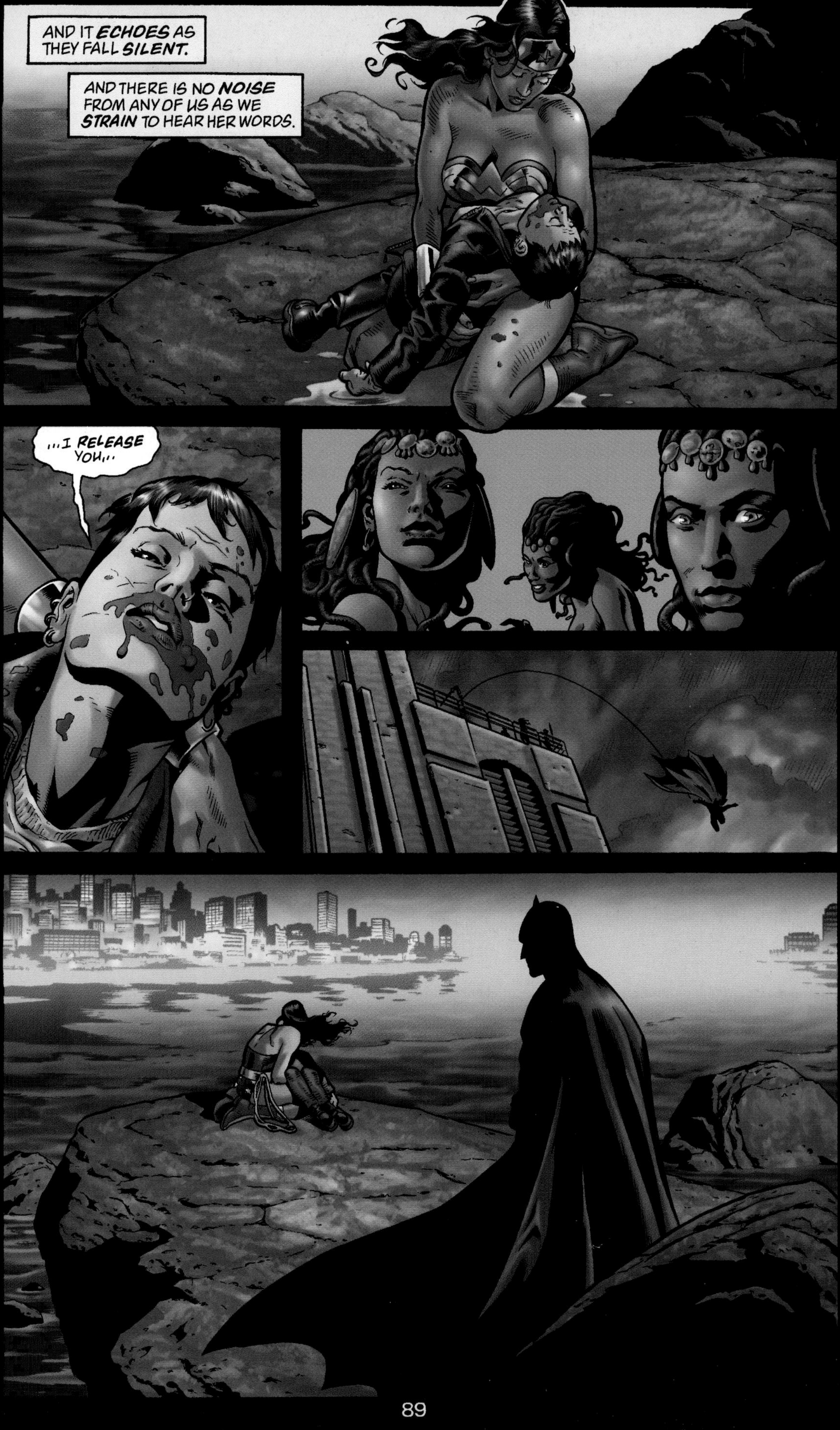

AND IT ECHOES AS THEY FALL SILENT.
AND THERE IS NO NOISE FROM ANY OF US AS WE STRAIN TO HEAR HER WORDS.
...I RELEASE YOU...

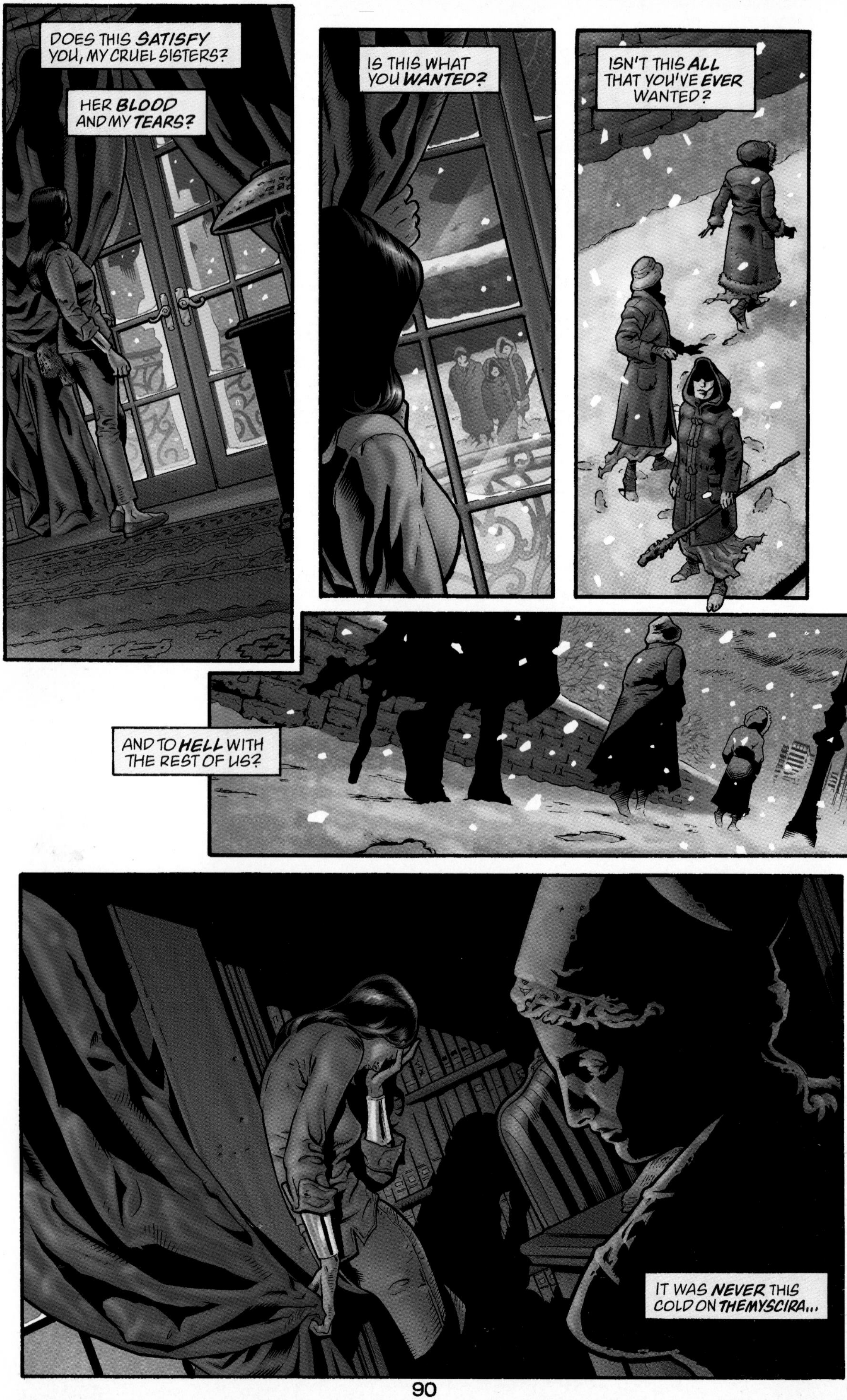
DOES THIS SATISFY YOU, MY CRUEL SISTERS?
HER BLOOD AND MY TEARS?
IS THIS WHAT YOU WANTED?
ISN'T THIS ALL THAT YOU'VE EVER WANTED?
AND TO HELL WITH THE REST OF US?
IT WAS NEVER THIS COLD ON THEMYSCIRA...

THE END

GREG RUCKA

Greg Rucka is the award-winning author of countless comics—including *Queen & Country, Whiteout,* and DETECTIVE COMICS—as well as the Atticus Kodiak series of novels published by Bantam Books. His work has been optioned for the large and small screen. THE HIKETEIA is his first published work featuring the DC icon Wonder Woman, and he hopes it will not be his last.

He lives in Portland, Oregon, with his wife, the writer Jennifer Van Meter, and their son Elliot, not a writer, but certainly full of good stories.

J.G. JONES

J.G. Jones is the Eisner Award-nominated illustrator of the Black Widow and Marvel Boy miniseries. He is also a painter and cover artist whom Hollywood continues to ignore.

He recently moved to New Jersey, where he has a breathtaking panoramic view of the Manhattan skyline, with his lovely wife Jann and several cats who possess miraculous secret powers.

WADE von GRAWBADGER

Wade von Grawbadger first gained attention for his work on STARMAN which won an Eisner Award for best serialized story for the "Sand and Stars" storyline. He was the regular inker on TITANS and *ShockRockets* before being offered, and jumping at, the chance to work with Greg and Jeff on THE HIKETEIA. He lives in Southern California and defies all logic, endangering his hands by playing indoor volleyball four times a week!

DAVE STEWART

Dave Stewart entered the comics field as a design intern at Dark Horse Comics. As a colorist, his projects include *Hellboy, Fray,* DOOM PATROL, BATMAN/NIGHTWING: BLOODBORNE and HUMAN TARGET: FINAL CUT.